Welcome to the magical island of Mykonos, a stunning destination in the heart of the Cyclades, Greece. Known for its golden sandy beaches, azure waters, iconic windmills, and charming white-washed buildings, Mykonos is a paradise that attracts travelers from all around the world. Whether you are seeking relaxation, adventure, romance, or a taste of the island's rich history and culture, Mykonos has something to offer everyone.

In this travel guide, we have carefully curated a selection of suggested itineraries to help you make the most of your time on this enchanting island. From exploring the essentials of Mykonos Town to discovering hidden beaches and experiencing the vibrant nightlife, these itineraries are designed to suit a variety of interests and preferences.

Additionally, we provide guidance on best things to do, top restaurants, where to stay, nightlife, the best beaches, island hopping, daily excursions and more.

Embark on a journey to the captivating island of Mykonos, where you will create unforgettable memories and discover the true essence of Greek island life. Let this guide serve as your compass, inspiring you to explore the unique beauty, charm, and allure that make Mykonos a truly unforgettable destination.

Contents

Introduction

1.1.   Welcome to Mykonos

Welcome to Mykonos, an enchanting Greek island that effortlessly blends traditional Cycladic charm with a modern, cosmopolitan vibe. Renowned for its vibrant nightlife, pristine beaches, and iconic windmills, Mykonos has become a popular destination for travelers seeking a luxurious and lively Mediterranean getaway.

1.2. Island Overview

Nestled in the heart of the Aegean Sea, Mykonos is part of the Cyclades archipelago. It covers an area of approximately 85.5 square kilometers (33 sq mi) and has a permanent population of around 10,000 residents. Mykonos Town (Chora), the island's capital, is a maze of whitewashed buildings, narrow cobblestone streets, and vibrant bougainvillea blossoms. The island's scenic coastline is dotted with numerous sandy beaches, crystal-clear turquoise waters, and hidden coves, perfect for sunbathing, swimming, and relaxation.

1.3. Brief History

Mykonos has a rich history dating back to the ancient times. According to mythology, it was named after its first ruler, Mykons, who was considered a descendant of the god Apollo. The island has been inhabited since the 5th millennium BC and was an important trading center during the Roman and Byzantine eras. In the 13th century, Mykonos fell under the rule of the Venetians, and later, the Ottomans. The island gained independence in 1821 during the Greek War of Independence and has since evolved into a thriving tourism destination.

Planning Your Trip

2.1. Best Time to Visit

Mykonos has a Mediterranean climate with hot, dry summers and mild winters. July and August are usually the hottest months. Mykonos has 300 days of sunshine a year. For more on Mykonos' climate check out the weather station <u>here</u>

The best time to visit Mykonos is between late May and early October, with the peak season occurring in July and August. During these months, you can expect warm, sunny weather and a lively atmosphere.

For a more relaxed experience, consider visiting during the shoulder months of May, June, September, and October, when the weather is still pleasant, and the crowds are smaller.

Best Time to Enjoy the Sun and Swimming at the Sea:
July, August, and September are the warmest months in Mykonos, with average temperatures of 26°C in July and 25°C in August. The sea begins to heat up in early July and reaches its warmest level in August. The sunniest period is in July, with the sun setting around 21:00, after which the days gradually become shorter.

Overall best time to travel to Mykonos: The best period to enjoy Mykonos is from June to September.

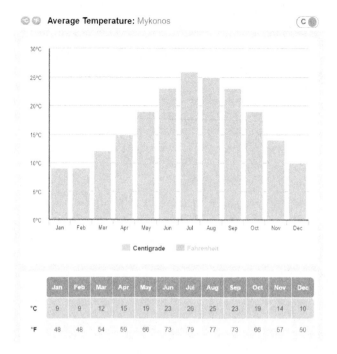

	Jan	Feb	Mar	Apr	May	Jun	Jul	Aug	Sep	Oct	Nov	Dec
°C	9	9	12	15	19	23	26	25	23	19	14	10
°F	48	48	54	59	66	73	79	77	73	66	57	50

Best Time to Visit Mykonos on a Low Budget: In Mykonos, the most affordable months for hotels and services are May and October. For instance, an average double hotel room that typically costs around 120 euros per day in July and August might be available for just 60 to 70 euros per day during these off-peak months.

Best Time to Visit Mykonos for the Nightlife: August is the prime month for experiencing Mykonos' vibrant nightlife. All clubs and bars are open, and numerous events are taking place, including beach concerts featuring famous Greek singers like Antonis Remos (particularly at Nammos beach bar in Psarou). During August, Mykonos is bustling with visitors, creating a lively atmosphere where everyone is in high spirits, embracing the summer mood.

Best Time to Visit Mykonos for Gay-Friendly Life: September is a popular month for gay-friendly couples to visit Mykonos. However, the island has been open-minded and accepting of everyone, regardless of their sexual preferences, for the past 40 years.

November to March: It's best to avoid visiting Mykonos from November through March. The sea is too cold for swimming, there are few locals on the island, and most shops are closed. Although it doesn't rain often, temperatures hover around 10°C, and strong winds make it uncomfortable to be outside.

Mykonos in April: In April, the sea remains cold and unsuitable for swimming. However, if the Easter holidays fall in April, many Athenians visit the island during Easter week, especially if the weather is good. Expect temperatures around 18°C. Prices are low, and most shops begin to open in April, but it's not the best month to visit Mykonos. According to the Greek Tourism Office, approximately 3,000 visitors arrive on the island by airplane in April, compared to 50,000 in June.

Mykonos in May: In May, the weather improves, with occasional heatwaves pushing temperatures up to 36°C, although average temperatures are typically around 25°C. The sea is still chilly, but with some bravery, you can swim. Beaches are pleasant but not crowded, and there may not be as much entertainment in May. If you're visiting Athens and want to spend a long weekend on a Greek island, Mykonos in May can be a good option, with prices generally lower than in June, July, and August.

Mykonos in June: June is a delightful month to visit Mykonos. The Holy Spirit long holidays in Greece, which occur sometime in June each year, draw many visitors to Mykonos for a short break. Hotel prices begin to rise, and most shops are open. The days are longer, with daylight lasting until around 8 PM. At least 50,000 tourists arrive in Mykonos by plane during June.

Mykonos in July: July and September are the two best months to visit Mykonos. Prices until the 20th of July aren't as high as in August, and while the island is busy, it's not as crowded as in August. Swimming is enjoyable, even though the sea isn't as warm as in August.

Mykonos in August: August is Mykonos' busiest month. Greeks typically vacation from the 1st to the 20th of August, and the island is teeming with both locals and tourists. Parties are in full swing, and all hotspots are open. However, you'll likely encounter heavy traffic, with travel times to beaches increasing due to congestion on the island's narrow roads. For example, a 15-minute trip from Mykonos Town to the beach could take up to 35 minutes. Prices are at their highest during this time, so it's essential to book well in advance. Don't expect to find a decent place at a reasonable price if you arrive in August without a reservation. The sea is at its warmest, making swimming particularly enjoyable.

Mykonos in September: September is an excellent month to visit Mykonos. The sea remains warm, and prices are lower than in August. There are still many visitors, particularly until the 15th of September. Daylight lasts until about 7:30 PM, allowing you to enjoy a less crowded island compared to August. However, if your primary goal is to party non-stop, August might be a better choice.

Mykonos in October: October marks the end of the tourist season in Mykonos. The weather and sea begin to cool down, and shops start closing for the season. Don't expect large crowds or lively parties on the island during this time. Visiting Mykonos for a long weekend while exploring Athens could be a pleasant option in October.

2.2. Visa Requirements

As a member of the European Union and the Schengen Agreement, Mykonos follows the same visa regulations as other Schengen countries. Visitors from non-Schengen countries may require a short-stay visa, depending on their nationality. It is essential to check the visa requirements for your specific country before planning your trip.

2.3. Transportation

Mykonos is easily accessible by air and sea. The island has an international airport with regular flights from Athens and other European cities during the summer months. Alternatively, you can take a ferry from Athens' Piraeus or Rafina ports. Once on the island, you can rent a car, scooter, or ATV to explore, or use the local bus and taxi services.

2.4. Currency and Budget Tips

The currency used in Mykonos is the Euro (€). The island is known for its high prices, so it's essential to plan your budget accordingly. While luxury hotels and fine dining can be costly, there are affordable accommodation and dining options available for budget-conscious travelers.

2.5. Language and Communication

Greek is the official language of Mykonos, but English is widely spoken in tourist areas. Learning a few basic Greek phrases can be helpful and appreciated by the locals.

2.6. Health and Safety

Mykonos is generally a safe destination for travelers. However, it is essential to take standard precautions, such as keeping your belongings secure and being aware of your surroundings. In case of a medical emergency, there are local clinics and a hospital available on the island. It is also recommended to have travel insurance for added protection.

2.7 Pros and Cons of Visiting Mykonos

Mykonos, a renowned European island destination, offers a unique blend of experiences for its visitors. Here's a quick overview of the pros and cons of visiting Mykonos:

Pros:

• Vibrant Atmosphere: Mykonos is known for its lively energy, making it a perfect destination for those looking to let loose and have a good time.

• Luxurious Accommodations: The island boasts some of the finest hotels in Greece, ensuring a comfortable and memorable stay for those who can afford it.

• Exceptional Service: Mykonos stands out for its hospitality, with top-notch service provided across the island.

• Stunning Beaches: With pristine white sand and crystal-clear waters, the beaches of Mykonos are truly breathtaking.

• Exciting Nightlife: The island is famous for its vibrant parties and bustling nightlife scene.

• Inclusivity: Mykonos is known for its open-mindedness and acceptance of diversity, including the LGBTQ+ community.

• Charming Main Village: The picturesque main village, Chora, offers a delightful experience for visitors to explore.

Cons:

• High Costs: Mykonos is known for its pricey accommodations, dining, and entertainment options.

• Limited Outdoor Activities: While the island is a haven for beach lovers, it may not be ideal for adventure-seekers as it lacks options for hiking, scuba diving, or other sports.

• Road Safety Concerns: Visitors should exercise caution when driving on the island, especially if renting a buggy car or other unconventional vehicles.

2.8 Tips for your trip to Mykonos

• Make sure to book your flights and hotels well in advance to secure a comfortable room at a reasonable price and an affordable flight. The touristic season in Mykonos starts in April and lasts until the end of October.

• Brace yourself for potentially bumpy boat rides. During the summer months (July and August), the local "Meltemi" wind, blowing from the northeast, can cause choppy seas. If you're prone to seasickness, consider avoiding small boat tours during this time.

- Don't forget to pack sunglasses and sunscreen to protect yourself from the sun.
- Mykonos Town is ideal for exploring on foot. Ladies, be cautious when walking on cobblestone streets in high heels; opt for flat shoes for a safer experience.
- Inquire at your hotel about wine-tasting excursions or other activities (see our guide for recommendations in Mykonos). Be sure to visit some of the lesser-known museums, which can be surprisingly captivating.
- Navigating Mykonos Town can be challenging, as some streets lack names. Don't hesitate to ask locals for directions if you get lost!
- Drive cautiously and at low speeds on the island's narrow roads.
- Bring a light jacket for nighttime strolls, as the sea breeze can make evenings chilly.
- Check the wind direction each morning to select the best beach for the day's conditions.
- Mykonos has two ports: the new port, where you're likely to arrive, and the old port, from which boats to Delos depart. A bus connects the new port to the town, and you can find the ports' locations on our map here.

2.9 How to Travel from Athens To Mykonos

To travel from Athens to Mykonos, you can choose between a flight (40 minutes), a fast ferry (2 hours and 10 minutes), or a slow ferry (5 hours). Ferries depart from either Rafina Port (35 km from Athens Center) or Piraeus Port (14 km from Athens Center).

Getting from Athens to Mykonos by ferry from Piraeus Port or Rafina Port:
To reach Piraeus, take metro line 1 (green line) across Athens and alight at the final stop. If arriving at Athens airport, catch the X96 Bus, which departs every 20 minutes from the airport bus station and takes about 70 minutes to reach the port. A taxi from the airport to the port

should cost around 35 euros, while a taxi from other parts of Athens will cost approximately 15-20 euros. The ferry trip from Piraeus takes around 5.5 hours (depending on the vessel and weather conditions), with timetables varying throughout the year. Trip costs start at 35 euros for economy class. Check schedules and prices before your trip **here.**

Rafina, located between Athens and Marathon, is the region's second-largest passenger port. To reach Rafina, take the bus from Mavromateon Street – Pedion Areos (a 10-minute walk from metro line 1 station "Victoria"). Buses depart every 15-45 minutes from 05:45 AM to 10:30 PM. The journey to Rafina's Port takes 1 hour, and a ticket costs 2.40 euros. Alternatively, you can take a taxi from Athens center to Rafina's port, which takes about 1 hour (depending on traffic) and costs around 35 euros.

Traveling from Athens International Airport directly to Rafina's Port: If you arrive at Eleftherios Venizelos Airport and wish to go to Rafina Port, you can take a bus located between exit 2 and 3 of the arrival hall. The journey takes about 30 minutes and costs 3 euros.

The ferry trip from Rafina takes around 4.5 hours (depending on the vessel and weather conditions), with timetables varying according to the time of year. Trip costs start at 30 euros for economy class travel. Check schedules and prices before your trip here.

For detailed information on bus and train timetables to and from the airport, check **here**

Getting from Athens to Mykonos by plane:

There are daily direct flights from Athens International Airport 'Eleftherios Venizelos' to Mykonos, with a flight duration of 40 minutes. Many airlines operate flights to and from Mykonos, with an increase in charter flights from various European cities during the high season (late April to September). Check a flight booking website like

Skyscanner for prices and timetables, as they can vary greatly depending on the time of year.

Five airlines offer direct flights from Athens to Mykonos: Aegean Airlines, Olympic Airways, Ryanair, Easyjet, and Elinair. If you book early, you can find fares between 50-60 USD per person. Last-minute bookings may cost up to 150 USD for a single flight from Athens to Mykonos. Visit http://www.viva.gr to check prices and timetables.

Athens has only one airport, Eleftherios Venizelos Airport, also known as AIA (Athens International Airport). It is located 40 km outside of Athens' city center, and it takes approximately 40 minutes to get there by taxi, metro, or bus. The taxi fare from central Athens to AIA ranges from 40 to 50 euros for up to 4 passengers in the same cab.

Cheapest Way to Get from Athens to Mykonos:

The most affordable ways to get from Athens to Mykonos include taking either a slow or fast ferry or opting for a low-cost airline flight. Here's an explanation:

There are two types of ferries that can transport you from Athens to Mykonos: slow and fast. Interestingly, the fast ferry can sometimes be cheaper than the slow one.

The fast ferry that departs at 07:15 in the morning from Rafina Port (not Piraeus Port) to Mykonos takes only 2 hours and 15 minutes and costs 22 Euros per person. In contrast, other ferries may take 4 hours and 30 minutes and cost 29 Euros per person.

So, the most cost-effective way to travel from Athens to Mykonos is by taking an early morning ferry from Rafina Port for just 22 euros per person, arriving in Mykonos in just a couple of hours.

As for flights, prices used to be quite high until a few years ago when low-cost airlines began operating between Athens and Mykonos. If you book your flight a couple of months in advance, you can find fares

15

ranging from 25 to 40 euros per person. For example, the table below shows that you can fly with Sky Express from Athens to Mykonos for only 38 Euros per person if you book a couple of months before your travel date.

2.10 How to Get from the Airport to the Center of Mykonos

Mykonos international airport is located 4 km (15') away from the town center. There are four ways to get to the city center, after your landing at the airport.

1. **Get a Taxi:** You can pick up a taxi at the taxi station which is located near the arrivals terminal. It may be difficult to find an available taxi, especially in the high season. The taxi will cost you 15 euros (from the airport to Mykonos Town). For extensive price list for other destinations, check here

2. **Get a Bus.** Actually, there is not frequent bus service connecting the airport with the town of Mykonos, and it is operating only in high season. It is better to look at the timetables, before your arrival, to see if you can catch a bus. The bus will cost you 1.60 euros.

3. **Rent a car.** You can find rent-a-car operators in the arrivals. It would be better to pre-book your car. Driving towards the town is easy; you have just to follow the signs. Have in mind that -if your hotel is in town- you cannot park your car there. You must use the parking lot at the port.

4. **Airport shuttle service.** Arrange with your hotel to have somebody to pick you up. They will be happy to help you, and they usually do it for free. This is the most convenient and easiest way.

2.11 Getting Around in Mykonos

You can navigate the island using the following methods:

-Bus

You can access the main tourist attractions and beaches by bus. There are three bus stations in Mykonos town, each serving different destinations. During the high season, buses depart as frequently as every 30 minutes, and there are also night buses available. The bus is the most affordable means of transportation in Mykonos, with ticket prices ranging between 1 and 2 euros. You can find bus timetables **here,** and consult the map **here** for the location of the bus stations. Keep in mind that there is no direct bus connection between the two bus stations, so you'll need to walk about 20 minutes from one station to the other.

Renting a Car or Motorbike:
The fastest way to explore Mykonos is by renting a car or motorbike. Numerous rental agencies are available, but it's a good idea to book your vehicle well in advance, especially during the busiest months. If you have a license, consider renting a motorcycle, as parking can be challenging. Drive cautiously on the island's narrow roads, maintain a low speed, and avoid overtaking. Always wear a seatbelt or helmet to avoid fines and, of course, don't drink and drive. There is a large, free parking lot at the "old port," just outside the town, where you can park for an unlimited time, and it's only a short walk away.

Taxi:
Taxis are a popular transportation option on the island. However, with only 30-40 taxis servicing the entire island, it can be challenging to find an available vehicle during the summer months. There is a taxi station in the town; consult the map here. You can find a comprehensive price list here.

Boat:
To visit beaches on the southern part of the island, you can take a "kaiki," a small boat. For more information on timetables, check here. There is also a boat service to Delos island. For additional information, visit this link.

Where to Stay in Mykonos: Beach or Town?

Deciding whether to stay in Mykonos town or near the best beaches in Mykonos (e.g., Psarrou, Paraga, Paradise, Super Paradise, Panormos, and Elia) is a pleasant dilemma to face during your vacation. To help you make your decision, here's a quick overview, with more detailed explanations provided later in this guide. Remember, Mykonos is a small island, so you can easily travel between locations no matter where you choose to stay.

• If you're single or traveling with friends, stay in Mykonos town.
• If you want to party, stay in Mykonos town.
• If you're a couple visiting Mykonos for the first time, stay in Mykonos town.
• If you're on your honeymoon, avoid the main town and choose a five-star hotel on the beach (see our post on the best areas and hotels for a honeymoon in Mykonos).
• If you're a family with kids, stay close to the beaches.
• If you prioritize relaxation and don't enjoy noise and parties, stay near the beaches.

When is the Beach Season in Mykonos?

Mykonos enjoys around 330 days of sunshine annually, but that doesn't guarantee beach-friendly weather year-round. The prime beach season runs from June to September. In March and April, the sea is typically too cold for swimming, unless you're exceptionally brave or hail from a colder climate like Siberia. May can be cool, but occasionally warm days make swimming possible. June is generally warm enough for swimming, while July, August, and early September are the hottest months with the warmest sea temperatures in Mykonos. October isn't ideal for beach visits, and swimming is generally not recommended from November through February. Consequently, if you visit Mykonos in April, May, or October, the beach areas may feel somewhat deserted compared to Mykonos town, making the town a more suitable accommodation choice during those months.

Here are the beach areas where you can stay in Mykonos, along with their respective distances from Mykonos town:

- Ornos Village and beach area: 3.3 km from Mykonos town (8 minutes driving time without traffic)
- Platis Gialos beach and village area: 4.4 km from Mykonos town (10 minutes driving time)
- Agios Ioannis village and beach area: 4.9 km from Mykonos town (12 minutes driving time)
- Paradise Beach Area: 5.8 km from Mykonos town (15 minutes driving time)
- Super Paradise Beach Area: 7.3 km from Mykonos town (18 minutes driving time)
- Paraga Beach Area: 5.6 km from Mykonos town (15 minutes driving time)
- Panormos beach and village area: 7 km from Mykonos town (20 minutes driving time)
- Elia beach area: 13 km from Mykonos town (27 minutes driving time)
- Kalafati beach area: 12.6 km from Mykonos town (21 minutes driving time)
- Agios Stefanos beach and village area: 5 km from Mykonos town (12 minutes driving time)

Mykonos has 25 beaches, some surrounded by small villages, while others are more secluded. The locations listed above are the best beach areas for accommodation in Mykonos.

Pros and Cons of Staying Near the Beach Areas:
Pros:
- Easy access to the beach: Wake up, have breakfast, and enjoy the water without needing to travel from Mykonos town.

- More relaxed atmosphere: The beach areas offer a more laid-back vibe compared to Mykonos town.
- Better value for money: Accommodations near the beach areas generally provide better value compared to those in Mykonos town.
- Ideal for honeymoon couples: The serene surroundings make beach areas a perfect choice for honeymooners.

Cons:
- Limited dining options: Beach villages have fewer restaurants compared to Mykonos town.
- Fewer shopping opportunities: Shopping options are more limited in beach areas compared to Mykonos town.
- Transportation to and from Mykonos town: You may need to take a bus or taxi to visit Mykonos town in the evening, which can be expensive (around 30 euros one way) and difficult to find during peak months (July and August), given the limited number of taxis on the island.
- Fewer nightlife options: The main party scene after 22:00 is in Mykonos town, so staying near the beach areas means fewer options for nightlife activities.

Where to Stay in Mykonos for a Group of Friends: Beach or Town?

If you and your friends are visiting Mykonos to party and have fun during the day and evening, it's best to choose Mykonos town as your base. During the day, you can take a bus from Mykonos town (Fabrika Bus stop) to one of the popular beaches on the island (e.g., Psarou, Super Paradise, Paradise, Paraga, Ornos, Panormos beach, etc.) and return in the afternoon. In the evening, you can easily enjoy the nightlife in Mykonos town and walk back to your accommodation without worrying about driving or finding a taxi.

After 22:00, the main party scene moves to Mykonos town, as beach parties at locations like Tropicana Bar at Paradise beach, Super Paradise Bar at Super Paradise beach, or Nammos at Psarrou beach begin to wind down.

During peak season in July and August, finding a taxi in Mykonos can be challenging due to the limited number of taxis (only 30 on the island) and high demand. Additionally, taxi fares can be quite expensive. Staying in Mykonos town allows you to avoid these transportation difficulties while still enjoying the best of the island's daytime and nighttime activities.

Where to Stay in Mykonos for Couples: Beach or Town?

As a couple, you might want to enjoy relaxing beach days, dine at lovely restaurants in the evening, take romantic walks, and enjoy cocktails at bars with beautiful views. If this describes your ideal vacation, then staying in Mykonos town is the best choice for you.

By basing yourselves in Mykonos town, you can easily take a bus to the beach during the day and return in the afternoon to prepare for a night out in town. Mykonos town offers a wide variety of restaurants, giving you plenty of choices for dining. It also has the largest selection of bars on the island, and you can enjoy romantic views from the bars in Little Venice.

Keep in mind that the bus service from Mykonos town to the beach areas usually stops at 12:00 am, depending on the month you're visiting. This means you may need to end your night early or take a taxi back, which could cost you around 30 euros each time.

Don't worry about missing out on privacy or quiet moments while staying in Mykonos town. You can still find romantic spots, less crowded bars, and your own little slice of paradise within the town. Additionally, shopping options are much better in Mykonos town compared to the beach areas.

3.1 The best areas to stay in Mykonos

When planning your trip to Mykonos, one of the first questions that may come to mind is, "What is the best area to stay in Mykonos?" In

21

this part of the guide, we'll cover the best areas to stay in Mykonos, including Mykonos Town, Ornos, Agios Stefanos, Platys Gialos, and Panormos. By the end of this guide, you'll be well-equipped to make the best decision based on your interests and preferences.

Keep in mind that there is no one-size-fits-all "Best Area to Stay in Mykonos." Your choice will depend on factors such as your budget, proximity to the beach or nightlife, and personal preferences.

For example, Mykonos Town has its fair share of detractors who dislike the noise, traffic, and crowds, particularly during the peak season of July and August. On the other hand, there are die-hard fans who love the bustling atmosphere and would never consider staying near the beach and driving to Mykonos Town in the evening, especially after indulging in a few drinks.

Before diving into the specifics of each area and their pros and cons, it's essential to familiarize yourself with the available options in terms of villages or areas and the best beaches in Mykonos.

What are the top areas/villages to stay in Mykonos?

The top four areas where most visitors choose to stay in Mykonos are Mykonos Town, Ornos, Platys Gialos, and Agios Stefanos. Other notable areas include Panormos, Ano Mera, and Kalafatis. To help you visualize the locations of these areas, refer to this map:

*The main areas to stay in Mykonos are Mykonos Town, Ornos, Platys Gialos, Agios Stefanos. You can open this map at Google maps, **here.***

As evident from the map, Mykonos is a relatively small island. The distance from Mykonos Town to Agios Stefanos is 3 km, Mykonos Town to Platis Gialos is around 4 km, and Mykonos Town to Ornos is 3.5 km.

3.2 Where are the best beaches in Mykonos island?

The most popular beaches in Mykonos are the following (ordered by the most popular):

1. Super Paradise Beach
2. Paradise Beach
3. Psarou Beach
4. Paraga Beach
5. Platis Gialos Beach
6. Agios Stefanos Beach
7. Kalo Livadi Beach
8. Ornos Beach
9. Kalafati Beach
10. Panormos Beach

23

11. Elia beach

Here is a map to help you understand where each beach is located:

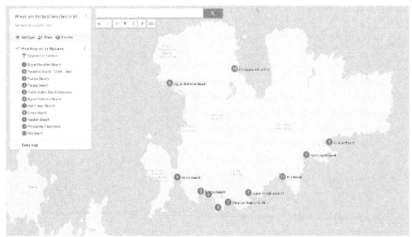

1Where the best beaches of Mykonos are located: Super Paradise, Paradise, Psarou, Paraga, Ornos beach, Platis Gialos Beach, Kalafati Beach, Agios Stefanos beach, Panormos Beach, Elia Beach.

You can view this map online at Google Maps, **here.**

Based on the two maps provided, it's clear that you'll need to do some traveling around Mykonos island to visit the many beautiful beaches spread across the area.

Now, let's examine the pros and cons of the best areas to stay in Mykonos island.

3.3 Staying in Mykonos Town (Chora)

A panoramic view of the harbor of Mykonos town (flickr/cc)

Mykonos Town, also known as "Chora" by the locals or simply "Mykonos," is the largest and most picturesque village on the island. The iconic images of windmills, white houses, and bustling narrow streets are all from this area.

If you choose to stay in Mykonos Town, a typical plan might involve heading to one of the popular beaches around 11:00 am to 12:00 pm and staying there until the afternoon, enjoying a light lunch. You would then return to Mykonos Town between 6:00 pm and 7:00 pm for dinner, followed by an evening stroll or visit to a bar/club.

Important Tip: During the high season (July 20th to August 20th), taxis are in high demand, as there are only 35 on the island. You may have to wait in long queues or struggle to find one.

Mykonos Town Pros:
• The island's buzz is centered here from the afternoon until late at night.
• The best bars, clubs, and restaurants on the island are located here.
• Mykonos Town is the prime spot for people-watching, as the rich and famous tend to visit during the evening.
• It's an excellent place to enjoy a morning coffee by the sea and continue people-watching.
• Known as "the island of the winds," Mykonos can get quite windy in August. The town's architecture provides a natural shield from strong winds.
• Parking, which used to be a nightmare, has been made easier with a large, public, free parking area at the old port, just 500 meters from Mykonos Town.

Mykonos Town Cons:

- Accommodation is generally more expensive compared to Ornos, Agios Stefanos, and other areas of Mykonos. During high season, you may struggle to find anything decent below 150 to 200 euros per night for a double room. If you want more luxury, expect to pay at least 300 to 400 euros per night for a 4 or 5-star hotel during peak season.
- The town gets noisy in the evenings due to the bustling crowds and parties. If you prefer a more relaxed atmosphere, consider staying in a different village.
- Cars are not allowed within Mykonos town, so you'll have to walk to your parking spot, which might be 10-15 minutes away.
- Mykonos Town lacks a beach. To reach the nearest beaches, you'll need to take a car, bus, or motorbike. The bus station where all buses depart towards the beaches is located in an open space area at the southern part of Mykonos town. Remember the tip about taxis in Mykonos, as well.

3.3.1 The Best Hotels in Mykonos Town

Here is a list of our recommended hotels in Mykonos Town, sorted by budget. Keep in mind that peak season runs from mid-July to late August, and during this period, prices in Mykonos are at least 30% more expensive than in June or September. It's difficult to find decent accommodation below 150 euros per night during peak season.

Best Luxury 5-Star Hotels in Mykonos Town (click on the links to check prices)
- Myconian Kyma Design Hotel
- Cavo Tagoo Mykonos
- Myconian Naia
- Kouros Hotel and Suites
- Bill & Coo Suites and Lounges
- Boheme
- Semeli
- Myconian Korali

Here is a map with the location of these 5-Star Hotels.

2 A map with the location of the best 5-star hotels in Mykonos Town

3.4 Staying in Ornos Village

3 Ornos Beach - Not an ideal beach if you look for some private space...

Ornos is the second most frequented village on the island after Mykonos Town and is definitely one of the best areas to stay in

Mykonos. It is close to Mykonos Town, at around 4 km or a seven-minute drive to the south.

Our perspective on staying in Ornos:
Although Ornos may not be as bustling as Mykonos Town, during peak season, the place is packed with people. In particular, Ornos Beach is crowded with umbrellas and sunbeds (as seen in the photo below). While Ornos is a convenient area to stay in due to its proximity to Mykonos Town, it doesn't stand out as particularly special. The village is decent, but you certainly won't enjoy walking around as much as you would in Mykonos Town. If you stay in Ornos, expect to visit Mykonos Town almost every afternoon. Be prepared to explore other beaches in the morning, such as Paragka Beach, Super Paradise Beach, and Psarou Beach, which are more appealing than Ornos Beach. We appreciate that Ornos is more affordable than Mykonos Town and offers quick access to many popular beaches on the island.

Ornos Pros:
• 10 to 20 percent cheaper than Mykonos Town for hotels and usually restaurants.
• It has a beach within walking distance.
• It is close to Psarrou and the Nammos bar (although you will still need a car to get there).
• Many nice restaurants are available.
• Platis Gialos Beach is nearby.
• Mykonos Town is just a 10-minute drive away when traffic is light.

Ornos Cons:
• The village lacks the picturesque charm of Mykonos Town.
• During the high season (July and August), the small road connecting Mykonos Town to Ornos becomes very busy, and it might take 20 to 25 minutes to cover the 4 km distance between Ornos and Mykonos.
• Compared to other beaches on Mykonos Island, Ornos Beach is just average.
• Parking can be challenging.

Here is a list of the best hotels to stay in Ornos:

The Best 5-Star Hotels to Stay in Ornos (click on the names to check the rates)
1. Kirini-My Mykonos Retreat
2. Kensho Boutique Hotel and Suites
3. Mykonos Blanc
4. Santa Marina – A luxury collection resort
5. Mykonos Ammos Hotel
6. Kivotos Mykonos

3.5 Staying in Platis Gialos

Platis Gialos beach
Take a look at the photo above to get an idea of the Platis Gialos area, which mainly consists of a beach with some luxury hotels and a few permanent residents.

Staying in Platis Gialos is one of the top four choices after Mykonos Town, Ornos, and Agios Stefanos. Don't expect to find a large village here; it's mostly vacation rentals and hotels situated around the beautiful Platis Gialos Beach.

Platis Gialos is also close to the popular Psarou Beach (a favorite among the rich and famous who visit the island, where you might end up paying 100 euros for a set of sunbeds).

The Best 5-Star Hotels in Platis Gialos (click on the names to check rates)
Here is a list with the best luxury hotels in Platis Gialos:
1. Nissaki Boutique Hotel
2. Myconian Ambassador Relais & Chateaux
3. Thalassa Boutique Hotel and Suites
4. Palladium Hotel
5. Branco Mykonos
6. Mykonos Dove Beachfront Hotel

3.6 The Best Budget Hotels in Mykonos

During the peak season (July - August), the average price per night for two people at a budget hotel is around 150 euros. In contrast, during the low and shoulder seasons, the average price per night for two people drops to 60-80 euros.

We had made a quick prices chart for the busiest months in Mykonos. So, take a look below for the price comparison chart.

Hotel	Rating	June	July	August	Link
Hotel Milena	9.3	€70	€117	€150+	Go
Nikos Rooms	8.3	€68	€109	€150+	Go
Makis Place	9.2	€89	€149	€150+	Go
Fraskoula's Beach	9.0	€65	€105	€149	Go
Sourmeli Garden Hotel	8.0	€91	€135	€144	Go
Asteri Hotel	8.9	€91	€140	€125	Go

Hotel Eleftheria	8.6	€80	€147	€150+	Go
Jason	9.2	€106	€143	€150+	Go
White Myth	8.5	€104	€150	€150+	Go

In order to get similar prices to our comparison chart, you would need to book at least several months in advance. Especially if you are considering visiting during the peak season.

As you may have already noticed, our selected budget hotels in Mykonos are highly rated and offer attractive prices during the peak season. These budget hotels range between 1 and 3 stars, so don't expect a luxurious room. However, we can assure you that each one of them will provide a comfortable stay during your holiday in Mykonos.

Additionally, some of these budget hotels are located outside of Mykonos Town. For this reason, we recommend checking their locations to ensure they won't cause any inconvenience during your stay.

Now, let's take a look at our budget hotel suggestions.

1. Hotel Milena (link to check rates):

Hotel Milena is a charming, traditional Greek-style hotel featuring plenty of white decor and open garden spaces. This 1-star, family-run hotel offers a warm and welcoming atmosphere.

Pros: The hotel is close to the bus stop and Mykonos Town, offers free transfers to/from the airport or port, has family rooms available, boasts a good location, and the staff is informative and helpful.

Cons: There is no complimentary water in the rooms, breakfast comes with an extra charge, rooms are on the small side, and bathrooms have an outdated design.

Star Rating: 1* | Guest Rating: 9.3 | Prices: June €70, August €150+

2. Nikos Rooms(click here to check rates):

Nikos Rooms is a traditional Greek-style hotel/hostel located less than 1 km from Mykonos Town and close to the airport, offering a convenient location for travelers.

Pros: The hotel features a pool and garden, provides free shuttle service to/from the airport, offers rooms with private bathrooms, and has a car rental service available.

Cons: Some guests have reported a dirty pool, a smelly and untidy environment, and occasional bugs in the bathrooms and rooms.

Star Rating: 2* | Guest Rating: 8.3 | Prices: June €68, August €150+

3. Makis Place (click here for rates:

Makis Place is a stylish hotel situated near the famous Mykonos Town port, just a 5-minute walk from Agios Stefanos Beach. It offers a swimming pool, sun terrace, and restaurant, providing guests with great value for their money. However, some drawbacks include free WiFi only in public areas, noise from the port and road, limited accessibility, and a late breakfast service. The hotel has a 2-star rating and a guest rating of 9.2, with prices starting at €89 in June and €150+ during August.

4. Fraskoula's Beach (click here for rates):

Located approximately 2.5 km from Mykonos Town, this family-run hotel is situated by Agios Stefanos Beach and offers stunning beach views. Guests can enjoy free WiFi, rooms with sea views, and close proximity to local taverns and spacious accommodations. However, the hotel lacks parking space, has poor public transportation access to the town, and charges extra for airport shuttle services. With a 1-star rating and a guest rating of 9, prices start at €65 in June and €149 in August.

5. Sourmeli Garden Hotel (click here for rates):

Sourmeli Garden Hotel is a traditional hotel with comfortable rooms and easy access to Mykonos Town, located near a beautiful beach. Guests can enjoy a good location, free car parking, beach access, and free WiFi. However, there may be noise from traffic, limited public transportation options, and an overpriced breakfast. The hotel has a 1-star rating and a guest rating of 8, with prices starting at €91 in June and €144 in August.

6. Asteri Hotel (click here for rates):

Asteri Hotel is a spacious and elegant hotel situated in Ornos, close to the local beach and just 2 km away from Mykonos Town. It offers daily public transportation, a swimming pool, proximity to shops and the beach, and very clean rooms. However, guests may experience noise from a busy road and find the beds to be very hard. The hotel has a 1-star rating and a guest rating of 8.9, with prices starting at €91 in June and €125 in August.

7. Hotel Eleftheria (click here for rates):

Hotel Eleftheria is situated near Ornos beach and is surrounded by a spacious garden with views of the Aegean Sea. Guests can enjoy its proximity to the beach, free WiFi, sea views, free parking, and a good location. However, the hotel is close to the main road, has untidy bathrooms, and can be difficult to find. With a 1-star rating and a guest rating of 8.6, prices start at €80 in June and €150+ in August.

8. Jason Hotel (click here for rates):

Jason Hotel, located less than 2 km from Mykonos Town, offers a peaceful atmosphere while being close to the main beaches. Guests can enjoy free WiFi, a swimming pool, free airport transfer, proximity to Mykonos Town, and modern rooms. However, the bar closes early, the breakfast is basic for the price, and there are not many activities around the hotel. With a 3-star rating and a guest rating of 9.2, prices start at €106 in June and €150+ in August.

9. White Myth:

White Myth, located in Mykonos Town, provides easy access to the beach and main tourist sights. Guests can enjoy a good location, modern rooms and bathrooms, free WiFi, and a guesthouse-style atmosphere. However, some rooms are small, some don't have windows, and the place can be difficult to find. With a 3-star rating and a guest rating of 8.5, prices start at €104 in June and €150+ in August.

3.7 A Map With All the Budget Hotels

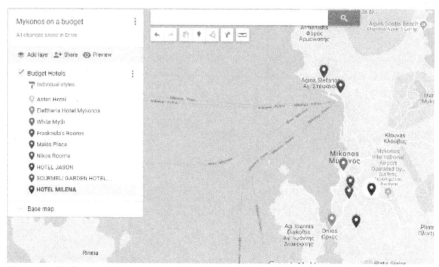

Get the full map **here**

Food and Dining

4.1. Traditional Mykonian Cuisine

The traditional Mykonian cuisine is an exquisite blend of Greek and Mediterranean flavors, with fresh, locally sourced ingredients taking center stage. Influenced by the island's rich history and maritime culture, Mykonian dishes are renowned for their simplicity, yet delicious and unique taste.

Some must-try Mykonian specialties include:
1. Kopanisti: A spicy, soft cheese made from fermented milk, typically served as a meze or appetizer with bread or rusks.
2. Louza: Thinly sliced, air-dried and spiced pork fillet, usually enjoyed as a meze or part of a charcuterie platter.
3. Amygdalota: Almond-based cookies, often flavored with rosewater or orange blossom water, and coated with powdered sugar. These sweets are a popular treat during festive occasions and celebrations.
4. Mostra: A traditional appetizer consisting of rusks topped with tomato, kopanisti cheese, oregano, and olive oil.
5. Ksinotyri: A tangy, fresh cheese made from goat or sheep's milk, often used in salads or enjoyed on its own.

When dining in Mykonos, you will find a plethora of restaurants and taverns serving these traditional dishes along with a variety of other Greek and international cuisines. From fine dining establishments to family-owned taverns and casual beachside eateries, there is a culinary experience for everyone on this enchanting island.

4.2. Best Restaurants

Mykonos boasts an array of fantastic restaurants, catering to various tastes and budgets. Here are some of the best restaurants on the island, offering a mix of traditional Greek cuisine, seafood, and international dishes.

1. **Kiki's Tavern:** This charming, family-run tavern is located in Agios Sostis and is known for its delicious grilled dishes, fresh salads, and stunning sea views. The laid-back atmosphere and friendly service make it a popular spot among both tourists and locals.

2. **Tasos Tavern,** located on the picturesque Paraga Beach, is a popular spot for locals and tourists alike who are seeking a true taste of Mykonos. Known for its exceptional seafood and traditional Greek dishes, Tasos Tavern offers a delightful dining experience complemented by a stunning beachfront setting. The welcoming atmosphere, combined with the fresh ingredients and skilled preparation, create a memorable culinary journey for all who visit. Whether you're enjoying a refreshing Greek salad, a plate of perfectly grilled octopus, or a glass of local wine, Tasos Tavern is a must-visit for anyone looking to savor the authentic flavors of Mykonos.

3. **Niko's Taverna:** A Mykonos institution, Niko's Taverna has been serving traditional Greek cuisine since 1967. Located in Mykonos Town, this bustling eatery is known for its fresh seafood, meze platters, and excellent wine selection.

4. **Scorpios:** This trendy beach club and restaurant in Paraga Beach offers a contemporary take on Mediterranean and Greek cuisine. With its bohemian decor, stunning sea views, and lively atmosphere, Scorpios is perfect for a leisurely lunch or dinner accompanied by signature cocktails.

5. **Funky Kitchen:** Located in Mykonos Town, Funky Kitchen is a modern restaurant with a creative menu that combines Greek and international flavors. The stylish interior, excellent wine list, and attentive service make it a favorite among foodies.

6. **Caprice Seafood Bar:** Overlooking the waterfront in Little Venice, Caprice Seafood Bar offers an unforgettable dining experience with its fresh seafood dishes, romantic atmosphere, and spectacular sunset views.

4.3 Reviews of 15 Selected Restaurants

Check out our comprehensive dining guide for Mykonos, a highly popular tourist destination that offers a wide range of dining options for all tastes and budgets. Our top 15 picks for where to eat in Mykonos have been carefully selected to provide you with an accurate overview of each restaurant's strengths and weaknesses, ensuring that you can make an informed choice for your next trip to the island.

	Restaurant	Rating	Location	Link
Luxury ($$$$)				
1.	Thioni	4.5	Mykonos town	Go
2.	Narcissus Mykonos	5	Mykonos town	Go
3.	Krama	4.5	Mykonos town	Go
4.	Lyo Bar	5	Mykonos town	Go
5.	M-eating	4.5	Mykonos town	Go
Mid-range ($$-$$$)				
6.	Jaipur Indian Palace	5	Mykonos town	Go
7.	Apaggio	4.5	Ornos	Go
8.	Bowl	4.5	Ornos	Go
9.	D'Angelo Mykonos	4.5	Mykonos town	Go
10.	To Apomero	4.5	Ornos	Go
Budget-friendly ($)				
11.	Popolo	4.5	Mykonos town	Go

12.	Local Mykonos	4.5	Mykonos town	Go
13.	Salt & Sugar Breakfast Lunch Dinner	4.5	Mykonos town	Go
14.	Il forno di Gerasimo	4.5	Mykonos town	Go
15.	Souvlaki Story Mykonos	4	Mykonos town	Go

Below, you will find two maps that display the locations of restaurants in Mykonos. Map 1 highlights the luxury and mid-range restaurant locations, while Map 2 shows the locations of 5 budget-friendly restaurants. To view the full map, please click here.

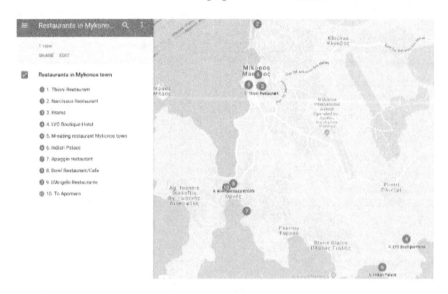

A Map with the Best Restaurants in Mykonos Town

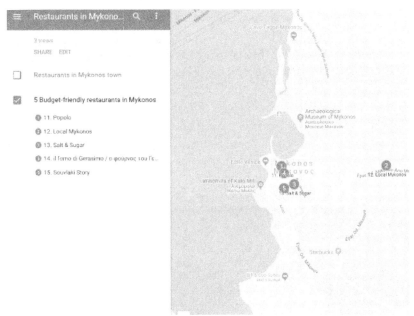

A map with the 5 best budget-friendly restaurants in Mykonos

1. Thioni Restaurant, Mykonos Town ($$$$)

Indoor area of Thioni resrtaurant

Thioni restaurant at Semeli hotel in Mykonos town is an excellent choice for a romantic dining experience in an antique and sophisticated setting. The restaurant offers indoor and outdoor seating options, and the celebrated Chef Nikos Palantzas serves signature Greek cuisine with a modern twist. Thioni restaurant serves seafood, Mediterranean, European, and Greek dishes at a price range of $23 - $57. The restaurant boasts attentive and knowledgeable service staff, a private atmosphere, and parking availability. Additionally, the menu includes vegetarian, vegan, and gluten-free options. However, keep in mind that this is a hotel restaurant, and the prices are comparably high. Free wifi is available, and you can visit their website at https://www.thionirestaurantmykonos.com/.

2. Narcissus Mykonos Restaurant, Mykonos Town ($$$$)

Sunset view at Narcissus restaurant.

Narcissus restaurant is a luxurious dining spot in Mykonos, known for its beautiful sunset view overlooking the hotel pool and the bay. They offer a signature Mediterranean dinner menu made with local ingredients and a nice selection of Greek wines. In 2018, the restaurant won the TripAdvisor Certificate of Excellence and has a tasting menu with exquisite meals. However, the menu is relatively expensive with a price range of $45-$159. Free wifi and parking are available on the premises. The restaurant's website is http://www.narcissusmykonosrestaurant.gr/.

3. Krama Restaurant, Mykonos Town ($$$$)

Indoor area of Krama restaurant

Located in the Semeli Hotel, the Krama restaurant offers a romantic evening dining experience with a modern interior and captivating views, albeit with a high price tag. The restaurant boasts a highly qualified staff and a charming veranda, where guests can enjoy the delicious Greek, Seafood, Mediterranean, European, and Contemporary cuisine. Krama also has a beautiful pool decorated with hundreds of small lights that adds to the romantic ambiance. In addition, the restaurant offers an extensive wine list and vegetarian and vegan options. The dishes are made by the renowned Chef Chrysanthos Karamolengos, and the restaurant also has a tasting menu. There are no major complaints about Krama, making it a must-visit destination for fine dining in Mykonos. Visit their website at https://www.kramamykonos.com/ for more information.

4. Lyo Bar Restaurant, Mykonos Town ($$$$)

Outdoor seating of Lyo Bar restaurant.

Located in the Lyo Boutique Hotel, the Lyo Bar restaurant is renowned for its high-quality seasonal seafood, including Bluefin tuna, red mullet, and sea bass. If you are a seafood enthusiast, this sushi bar is a must-visit, with many reviewers claiming it serves the best sushi they have ever tasted. The restaurant has won a TripAdvisor Certificate of Excellence in 2018 and offers a peaceful atmosphere without loud music. The staff is attentive, and vegetarian, vegan, and gluten-free options are available on the menu. Free off-street parking and WiFi are also available. The price range is $34 to $113. The restaurant's website is https://www.lyomykonos.com/.

5. M-eating Restaurant, Mykonos Town ($$$$)

M-eating restaurant from outside.

M-eating is a popular restaurant in Mykonos that serves local and fusion Mediterranean cuisine. The restaurant has a charming veranda with a relaxing ambiance, overlooking the street. Due to its popularity, it's recommended to make a reservation, especially during high season. M-eating has received numerous positive ratings from customers, making it a popular choice for visitors to the island. The staff is very attentive, and the restaurant offers vegetarian, vegan, and gluten-free options. The prices are reasonable, with a range of $28-$68 for dinner. M-eating has been awarded the Travelers' Choice 2018 Winner on TripAdvisor. The restaurant only serves dinner.

6.Jaipur Indian Palace, Mykonos Town ($$-$$$)

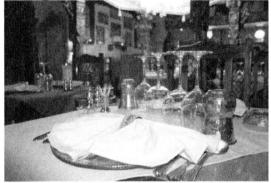

Located in the famous area of Mykonos, near Cavo Paradiso and Paradise Beach, Jaipur Palace restaurant offers exotic Indian and Asian cuisine in a colorful atmosphere with Indian music. The menu includes lunch, dinner, brunch, and late-night meals, with a price range that is not too expensive but not too cheap either, ensuring the quality of the dishes. The restaurant has a main hall with a capacity of 150 people, and a separate hall for gatherings and parties of up to 100 people. Vegetarian options are also available on the menu, and delivery and takeout services are offered. The restaurant provides parking, but its location between two clubs can make it a little noisy at times. Website: https://www.jaipur-palace.gr/en/mykonos.

7. Apaggio Restaurant, Ornos ($$-$$$)

Apaggio restaurant outdoor seating.

Apaggio restaurant is located just a five-minute walk from Ornos beach and boasts a beautiful setting right by the sea. With two main seating areas, one inside the building and one on the water's edge, this restaurant is quite popular among the locals and is famous for its generous portions. The menu features fresh seafood caught right from the sea, along with vegetarian-friendly, vegan, and gluten-free options. Apaggio has received a Certificate of Excellence on TripAdvisor and offers a stunning view of Ornos beach. However, the restaurant can get crowded at times. Prices range from $23 to $68. Website: https://apaggio.gr/

8. Bowl Restaurant, Ornos ($$-$$$)

Indoor area of Bowl restaurant

Bowl is a contemporary restaurant that caters primarily to those who are health-conscious and follows a vegetarian or gluten-free diet, which is prepared using local ingredients. This restaurant is owned and operated by an Australian couple who are passionate about Greece and have always wanted to move to Mykonos. You can indulge in tasty organic meals and juices in a modern setting. The restaurant also has an outdoor seating area, free off-street parking, accepts digital payments, and offers free Wi-Fi. With high ratings and fair prices, it is ranked #2 of 18 restaurants in Ornos.

9. D'Angelo Mykonos Restaurant, Mykonos town ($$-$$$)

Outdoor seating of D'Angelo Mykonos restaurant.

If you're looking for Mediterranean-Italian cuisine in a cozy and relaxing atmosphere, D'Angelo Mykonos is the place to go. Located near the famous Windmills of Mykonos, the restaurant has an expanded outdoor area where you can enjoy the beautiful view. With many positive reviews, it is quite popular among tourists. The attentive staff, friendly environment, and digital payments accepted are some of the pros of this restaurant. They also offer delivery and takeout options, and free wifi is available. However, during high season, customers may experience wait times for service, and some customers have complained that the non-smoking area is not properly separated. The price range is reasonable, ranging from $14 to $34. The restaurant has won a Certificate of Excellence on TripAdvisor for three consecutive years from 2015-2017. Check out their Facebook page for more information.

10. To Apomero Restaurant, Ornos ($$-$$$)

The seating area of To Apomero restaurant.

To Apomero restaurant is a cozy and comfortable eatery that offers a variety of cuisines, including Greek, seafood, and Mediterranean dishes. The relaxed setting and friendly staff create a comfortable and welcoming atmosphere. Many customers have rated this restaurant as a must-visit when in Ornos, and it has earned a TripAdvisor Certificate of Excellence for 2017-2018. The staff is attentive and accommodating, even during peak season when the restaurant is typically full. The restaurant offers free Wi-Fi, and vegetarian, vegan, and gluten-free options are available. While the restaurant's location may not be as convenient as others in Ornos, there are no significant complaints about the establishment.

11. Popolo Restaurant, Mykonos Town ($)

Entrance and outdoor seating area of Popolo restaurant.

Popolo café is a casual restaurant that offers breakfast, lunch, and pastries. You can enjoy a variety of dishes such as sandwiches, fresh salads, and Italian cuisine. The café is also well-known for its Greek yogurts with honey and fruits, and a selection of coffee, juices, cakes, and croissants. The food is tasty and affordable, and the staff is friendly and attentive. However, during peak hours, the café may get very busy, and you may have to wait for a while. The café also offers free Wi-Fi to its customers.

12. Local Mykonos Restaurant, Mykonos Town ($)

Indoor seating area of Local Mykonos restaurant.

Local Mykonos is a popular street food restaurant that serves traditional Greek souvlaki, a local favorite made with small pieces of meat, tomatoes, onions, fries, tzatziki, and wrapped in a lightly grilled pita bread. The restaurant offers budget-friendly meals and has high ratings for its service and value. Located near the main road of Mykonos, it has easy access and also provides free parking. The restaurant has a delivery service to every place in Mykonos and vegetarian-friendly options are available. With a helpful staff and friendly environment, Local Mykonos is a great choice for a quick and tasty break during your vacation.

13. Salt & Sugar Breakfast Lunch Dinner, Mykonos Town ($)

Inside Salt & Sugar restaurant.

Salt & Sugar is a small, lovely restaurant with many positive reviews from previous customers who said they would visit again. The restaurant is located in a peaceful corner, but you will not feel isolated. Salt & Sugar is always busy due to its reasonable prices and positive, friendly staff. The restaurant's most popular desserts are Greek yogurt and homemade "baklava." With a focus on Mediterranean, Cafe, European, and Greek cuisines, the restaurant also offers vegetarian, vegan, and gluten-free options. It has an outdoor seating area, free wifi, and accepts digital payments. However, some customers have complained about slow service during busy times. Salt & Sugar is a TripAdvisor Certificate of Excellence 2018 winner.

14. Il forno di Gerasimo Restaurant, Mykonos town ($)

Inside il forno di Gerasimo restaurant.

Il forno di Gerasimo is a bistro-café located in Mykonos town, famous for its homemade pizza, traditional pies, sandwiches, and paninis. It is a cozy place to stop for a quick breakfast or lunch during your vacation. The restaurant specializes in making fresh homemade baked dishes, so if you enjoy bakery, this is the right place for you. Il forno di Gerasimo has received a Certificate of Excellence 2017-2018 on TripAdvisor and is also ranked #1 of 6 bakeries in Mykonos town. The restaurant offers outdoor seating, free Wi-Fi, and reasonable prices that do not compromise the food quality.

15. Souvlaki Story Mykonos, Mykonos town ($)

Indoor seating area of Souvlaki Story restaurant.

Located in the center of Mykonos town, Souvlaki Story is a budget-friendly restaurant serving delicious Greek fast food. Popular for their gyros and souvlaki with pita bread, this cozy bistro-café is perfect for a quick and affordable meal. They also offer vegetarian and vegan options for those with dietary restrictions. With a Certificate of Excellence 2017-2018 from TripAdvisor, visitors have praised the tasty food and polite staff. However, the restaurant can get quite crowded during the high season. Prices range from $2 to $20, making it an excellent choice for budget-conscious travelers. Website: http://www.souvlakistory.com/

4.4 Eat like a Greek

Greece offers fantastic food, with local vegetables, cheeses, and meat. Although the menu could be huge and cover every passion you may have, here is a list of the must-try dishes in Greece.

Try these amazing Greek Food Starters:

Tzatziki

Tzatziki is a Greek sauce that you can try with grilled meats or as a dip with bread. Tzatziki is made of strained yogurt which comes from sheep or goat milk, and it is mixed with garlic, salt, cucumbers and olive oil. You may add mint, dill or parsley. Try it with bread, fried potatoes, and grilled meat or grilled fish. And get a mint for your breath afterward

Melitzanosalata (eggplant salad).

Melitzanosalata is a traditional Greek dish made from roasted eggplants, garlic, olive oil, lemon juice, and parsley. It is a popular meze (small dish) that can be found in many tavernas throughout Greece. The dish is typically served as a dip alongside bread, crackers, or pita bread, but it can also be used as a side dish for meat or fish. Melitzanosalata is a healthy and flavorful option for vegetarians and vegans, and it is rich in antioxidants and fiber. The dish has a smoky flavor due to the roasted eggplants and a tangy taste from the garlic and lemon juice. Melitzanosalata is easy to prepare and is a perfect addition to any Mediterranean-inspired menu.

Ntolmadakia

Ntolmadakia, also known as dolmades or stuffed grape leaves, are a popular Greek appetizer. They are made by filling grape leaves with a

mixture of rice, herbs, and occasionally minced meat, and then rolling them tightly into little parcels. The parcels are then boiled or steamed until the filling is cooked and the grape leaves are tender.

Ntolmadakia are typically served cold or at room temperature, and are often accompanied by a dollop of yogurt or tzatziki sauce. They can be found in most Greek restaurants and are a staple in traditional Greek cuisine.

The origins of ntolmadakia can be traced back to the Ottoman Empire, where they were known as dolma. The word dolma means "stuffed" in Turkish and refers to a wide range of stuffed dishes, including grape leaves, vegetables, and fruits. Over time, the dish spread throughout the Mediterranean and Middle East, where it took on different variations and local flavors.

Today, ntolmadakia are enjoyed not only in Greece but in many other countries around the world. They are a flavorful and healthy appetizer that is perfect for sharing with friends and family.

Fried potatoes (Greek, French fries)

Make sure you get the fresh Greek, French fries. Some restaurants serve pre-fried ones, which are nowhere close to the original ones. Ask before you order.

Greek Salad

Greek salad, also known as Horiatiki salad, is a popular dish in Greek cuisine. It is a refreshing and healthy salad made with fresh vegetables, typically including tomatoes, cucumbers, onions, green peppers, and olives. Feta cheese is also a key ingredient in Greek salad, providing a salty and tangy flavor that complements the vegetables well.

The dressing for Greek salad is usually made with olive oil, red wine vinegar, lemon juice, garlic, salt, and pepper. Some variations may also include herbs such as oregano or basil. The dressing is drizzled over the salad just before serving, allowing the flavors to meld together.

In Greece, Greek salad is often served as a side dish or appetizer, but it can also be a light meal on its own, especially during the hot summer months. It is a nutritious and low-calorie option, packed with vitamins and antioxidants from the fresh vegetables and healthy fats from the olive oil and feta cheese.

Greek salad has become popular around the world, with many variations and adaptations to local ingredients. However, the classic combination of fresh vegetables, feta cheese, and olive oil remains a staple of Mediterranean cuisine and a favorite of salad lovers everywhere.

Spinach and cheese pie

Spinach pie, also known as spanakopita, is a popular savory Greek pastry made with spinach, feta cheese, onions, eggs, and phyllo pastry. The filling is usually made by sautéing chopped spinach and onions with olive oil, then mixing it with crumbled feta cheese and beaten eggs. The mixture is then layered between sheets of phyllo pastry, which are brushed with olive oil to make them crispy and golden. The pastry is typically served as a snack, appetizer or a light meal, and it can be enjoyed hot or cold.

Cheese pie, or tiropita, is another popular Greek pastry that can be found in bakeries and cafes throughout Greece. It is made with a similar phyllo pastry as the spinach pie, but the filling is made with a mixture of feta cheese, ricotta cheese, eggs, and butter. The cheese mixture is layered between the sheets of phyllo pastry, which are then baked in the oven until they are golden and crispy. Cheese pie is often served as a breakfast or snack and can be enjoyed hot or cold.

Both spinach pie and cheese pie are popular choices for those who follow a vegetarian or Mediterranean diet. They are tasty and nutritious options, rich in protein and healthy fats. They can also be made in various sizes and shapes, such as small bite-sized pies or larger family-sized pies. Overall, these traditional Greek pastries are a delicious and convenient way to enjoy a quick and satisfying meal or snack.

Kolokithokeftedes (grilled zucchini balls)

Kolokithokeftedes, also known as zucchini fritters or patties, are a popular appetizer in Greek cuisine. These delicious fritters are made with grated zucchini mixed with onion, fresh herbs (such as dill and mint), and feta cheese, which are then formed into small patties and fried until crispy.

The name "kolokithokeftedes" comes from the Greek words "kolokithi," which means zucchini, and "keftedes," which refers to meatballs or patties. However, unlike traditional keftedes made with meat, kolokithokeftedes are a vegetarian option that is both tasty and healthy.

Zucchini fritters are commonly served as an appetizer or meze in Greece and can be found in many tavernas and restaurants. They are typically served with tzatziki sauce or a squeeze of fresh lemon juice, which adds a tangy flavor to the dish.

Kolokithokeftedes are not only delicious but also a great source of vitamins and nutrients. Zucchini is rich in antioxidants, potassium, and fiber, which are essential for maintaining good health. In addition, the feta cheese used in the recipe provides a good source of protein and calcium.

Main Courses:
Souvlaki (sticks with pork meat, grilled)

Souvlaki is a popular Greek dish made from small pieces of meat (usually pork, chicken, lamb or beef) that are skewered and grilled. The word "souvlaki" comes from the Greek word "souvla", which means skewer.

The meat is marinated with olive oil, lemon juice, herbs, and spices, giving it a delicious Mediterranean flavor. Once the meat is marinated, it is skewered and grilled over charcoal until it is cooked to perfection. The souvlaki is usually served on a plate or in a pita bread, accompanied by tomatoes, onions, and a variety of sauces such as tzatziki (a yogurt and cucumber dip), mustard, or ketchup.

Souvlaki is a popular street food in Greece and can be found at almost every taverna or grill house. It is also a staple at Greek festivals and celebrations. In addition to the traditional meat options, vegetarian souvlaki made with grilled vegetables, such as eggplant, zucchini, and peppers, is also a popular option.

Souvlaki is not only a delicious and satisfying dish but also a healthy one. The grilled meat and vegetables provide a good source of protein, vitamins, and minerals, while the use of olive oil and herbs make it a heart-healthy option. Souvlaki is a dish that truly represents the essence of Greek cuisine and is loved by locals and tourists alike.

Paidakia (lamb chops)

Paidakia is a popular dish in Greek cuisine that consists of lamb chops grilled or roasted with various herbs and spices. The dish is usually served with lemon wedges, roasted vegetables, and potatoes.

The lamb used in this dish is typically sourced from free-range or grass-fed sheep, which gives it a distinct flavor that sets it apart from other types of meat. The meat is marinated for several hours before cooking to infuse it with flavor and tenderness.

The marinade can vary depending on the region and the cook's personal preference, but it often includes ingredients such as olive oil, lemon juice, garlic, oregano, thyme, and rosemary. The lamb chops are then grilled or roasted to perfection, resulting in a juicy and flavorful meat that is crispy on the outside and tender on the inside.

Paidakia is a popular dish served at Greek tavernas and restaurants, often accompanied by a glass of red wine. It is a favorite among locals and tourists alike and is an excellent representation of the bold and hearty flavors that Greek cuisine is known for.

Moussaka

Moussaka is a popular dish in Greek cuisine that is made with layers of eggplant, potatoes, and seasoned ground beef or lamb, topped with a creamy bechamel sauce and baked until golden brown. The dish is often served as a main course and is a staple of Greek tavernas and restaurants.

The preparation of moussaka can vary depending on the region and personal preferences. Some recipes may include zucchini or other vegetables in addition to the eggplant and potatoes, while others may omit the meat or use a different type of meat.

To prepare moussaka, the eggplant and potatoes are typically sliced and fried in olive oil until they are tender and lightly browned. The meat is seasoned with herbs and spices such as oregano, cinnamon, and nutmeg, and is cooked until browned. The bechamel sauce is made with butter, flour, and milk, and is seasoned with grated nutmeg and salt.

Once all the components are prepared, the moussaka is assembled in layers in a baking dish. The bottom layer is typically the eggplant and potato slices, followed by a layer of the seasoned meat, and then another layer of eggplant and potatoes. The dish is then topped with the creamy bechamel sauce and baked in the oven until the top is golden brown and the dish is heated through.

Moussaka is a hearty and flavorful dish that is often served with a side salad or crusty bread. It is a perfect dish for a comforting family meal or for entertaining guests.

Pastitsio

Pastitsio is a popular Greek dish made with pasta, meat sauce, and a creamy béchamel sauce. It is similar to the Italian dish lasagna, but with Greek flavors and ingredients. The bottom layer is made up of tube-shaped pasta, such as penne or ziti, which is then topped with a flavorful meat sauce. The meat sauce typically includes ground beef or lamb, onions, garlic, and tomatoes, seasoned with cinnamon and other spices.

The next layer is a creamy béchamel sauce, which is made by cooking butter, flour, and milk together until it thickens. Cheese is often added to the béchamel sauce to give it extra flavor and richness. Once the béchamel sauce is ready, it is poured over the pasta and meat sauce to create a thick, creamy layer on top.

The dish is then baked in the oven until it is golden brown and bubbly. It is typically served hot, either as a main dish or as a side dish, and is often accompanied by a Greek salad and a glass of red wine. Pastitsio is a hearty, comforting dish that is popular throughout Greece, and is a favorite of many Greek families.

Fish (e.g. ask for Barbounia, Koutsomoures, which are red fried fish)

Barbounia and Koutsomoures are two popular types of fish found in Greek cuisine.

Barbounia, also known as red mullet, is a small, delicate fish with a distinctive flavor. It is typically grilled or fried and served with lemon, olive oil, and fresh herbs. In Greek cuisine, barbounia is often served whole, with the head and tail still intact. It is considered a delicacy and is often served on special occasions or as part of a festive meal.

Koutsomoures, also known as black mullet, is another popular fish in Greek cuisine. It has a firm, white flesh and a mild flavor. Koutsomoures is often grilled or fried and served with a variety of side dishes, including lemon potatoes, salad, or tzatziki. It is also a popular fish for fish soup, which is a common dish in Greek cuisine.

Both barbounia and koutsomoures are widely available in Greece and can be found on the menu of many traditional tavernas and seafood restaurants. They are often served as part of a mezze platter or as a main course. As with all seafood in Greece, they are typically served fresh and cooked simply, allowing the natural flavors of the fish to shine through.

Spaghetti with Lobster (*Astakomakaronada* in Greek)

Spaghetti with Lobster, also known as Astakomakaronada in Greek, is a luxurious and flavorful pasta dish that is popular in Greece and many Mediterranean countries. It is a seafood-based pasta dish made with fresh lobster meat, tomato sauce, garlic, white wine, and herbs like basil and parsley. The pasta used in this dish is typically spaghetti, but other long and thin pasta varieties like linguine and fettuccine can also be used.

To prepare Astakomakaronada, the lobster is first cooked in boiling water and then removed from the shell. The meat is then cut into small pieces and sautéed in olive oil with garlic and chili flakes to give the dish a bit of heat. The tomato sauce is added next, along with white wine and herbs, and simmered for a few minutes to infuse all the flavors together.

Meanwhile, the spaghetti is cooked until al dente, drained, and then added to the lobster tomato sauce mixture. The pasta is tossed in the sauce until it is fully coated and the flavors are well combined. The dish is then served hot, garnished with some fresh herbs like basil or parsley.

Astakomakaronada is a popular dish in coastal towns and islands of Greece, where fresh seafood is abundant. It is often served in upscale restaurants and is considered a delicacy due to the use of fresh lobster meat, which can be quite expensive. It is a rich and flavorful dish that is perfect for special occasions or romantic dinners.

Soutzoukakia – spiced meatballs in tomato sauce

Soutzoukakia is a popular Greek dish consisting of spiced meatballs in a rich tomato sauce. The meatballs are made of ground beef or pork, mixed with spices such as cumin, cinnamon, and garlic, and shaped into elongated, sausage-like forms. They are then cooked in a tomato sauce made with onions, garlic, tomatoes, and sometimes red wine.

The name "soutzoukakia" comes from the Turkish word "sucuk," which means sausage. The dish has Ottoman roots, as it was introduced to Greece during the Ottoman Empire's rule. However, over time, the Greeks have made this dish their own by adding their own unique twist to the recipe.

Soutzoukakia is often served with rice or potatoes, and sometimes with a side of Greek yogurt to balance out the spiciness of the dish. It is a hearty and comforting dish that is perfect for a cozy family dinner or a gathering with friends.

In Greece, soutzoukakia is a popular dish that can be found in many restaurants and tavernas. It is also a common homemade dish, with each family having their own unique recipe and way of preparing it. Soutzoukakia is a dish that has stood the test of time and remains a beloved staple of Greek cuisine.

Gemista (vegetables, usually tomatoes or pepper, stuffed with rice)

Gemista is a traditional Greek dish that features vegetables, usually tomatoes or peppers, stuffed with a flavorful mixture of rice, herbs, and sometimes ground meat. This dish is popular in the summer months when vegetables are abundant, and is often served as a main course or as part of a mezze platter.

To prepare gemista, the vegetables are first hollowed out and then filled with a mixture of rice, onion, garlic, parsley, dill, and sometimes ground beef or pork. The stuffed vegetables are then arranged in a baking dish, topped with olive oil and tomato sauce, and baked in the oven until tender and golden.

Gemista is a versatile dish and can be made with a variety of vegetables, including zucchini, eggplant, and potatoes. It can also be adapted to suit different dietary requirements, such as by using quinoa instead of rice or omitting the meat for a vegetarian or vegan version.

In Greece, gemista is often served with a side of feta cheese and crusty bread for dipping in the tomato sauce. It is a comforting and hearty dish that is perfect for sharing with family and friends, especially during the warm summer months.

Desserts you should try in Greece:
Galaktompoureko (milk pie)

Galaktompoureko, also known as milk pie, is a traditional Greek dessert made with layers of crispy phyllo pastry and a creamy custard filling. The custard is usually made with milk, sugar, semolina, cornstarch, eggs, and vanilla extract, and sometimes flavored with lemon zest.

To make galaktompoureko, the phyllo pastry is brushed with butter or olive oil and layered in a baking dish. The custard filling is then poured over the top and the dish is baked in the oven until the pastry is golden brown and crispy. Once baked, a simple syrup made with sugar, water, and lemon juice is poured over the top to add sweetness and moisture to the dessert.

Galaktompoureko is usually served cold, and can be garnished with ground cinnamon or powdered sugar. It is a popular dessert in Greece and can be found in most Greek bakeries and restaurants. The dessert is often served on special occasions, such as Easter and Christmas, but is also enjoyed year-round.

Revani

Revani is a traditional Greek dessert made of semolina flour, sugar, and eggs, drenched in a sweet syrup. It is typically served cold and garnished with chopped nuts, such as pistachios or almonds. Revani is a popular dessert in Greece and is often served at special occasions such as weddings, baptisms, and other celebrations.

To make Revani, a batter is made by combining semolina flour, sugar, eggs, milk, butter, baking powder, and vanilla extract. The batter is poured into a baking dish and baked in the oven until golden brown. While the cake is still hot, a sweet syrup made of sugar, water, lemon juice, and honey is poured over it, allowing the cake to soak up the syrup and infuse it with its sweet flavor.

Revani is a light and fluffy cake with a slightly grainy texture due to the use of semolina flour. The syrup gives the cake a sweet and tangy flavor, while the nuts provide a crunchy contrast to the soft cake. Revani can be served as a dessert after a meal or as a sweet snack with coffee or tea. It is a beloved dessert in Greece and is enjoyed by locals and visitors alike.

Halva

Halva is a sweet, dense confection made from tahini (ground sesame paste) and sugar or honey. It is a traditional dessert found in many Middle Eastern and Mediterranean cuisines, including Greek, Turkish, and Arabic. There are many variations of halva, but the basic ingredients remain the same.

To make halva, the tahini and sugar or honey are mixed together and cooked over low heat until the sugar has dissolved and the mixture has thickened. Nuts or other flavorings such as vanilla or cinnamon may be added at this stage. The mixture is then poured into a dish, smoothed out, and left to cool and set.

Halva is typically served in small slices or cubes, and can be enjoyed on its own or with tea or coffee. It is also often used as an ingredient in other desserts, such as ice cream or cake. Halva has a unique texture that is dense and crumbly, and a sweet, nutty flavor that is popular with many people. It is a great dessert option for those who are looking for a sweet treat that is not too heavy or rich.

Baklava

Baklava is a sweet pastry made of layers of filo pastry, chopped nuts (usually walnuts or pistachios), and sweet syrup or honey. It is a popular dessert in Greece, Turkey, and other parts of the Middle East and Mediterranean.

The exact origin of baklava is debated, but it is believed to have been created in the Ottoman Empire during the 15th century. Baklava is now enjoyed in various forms throughout the world, with each region putting its own spin on the recipe.

To make baklava, layers of filo pastry are brushed with melted butter or oil and then layered with a mixture of finely chopped nuts and sugar. The layers are then baked until golden brown and crispy. Once removed from the oven, the pastry is soaked in a sweet syrup or honey, allowing the flavors to blend and the pastry to absorb the moisture.

Baklava can be served in various shapes and sizes, such as large trays cut into squares or individual portions. It is often garnished with chopped nuts or a dusting of cinnamon or powdered sugar.

In Greece, baklava is commonly enjoyed during special occasions and celebrations, such as weddings and religious holidays. It is also a popular treat in cafes and pastry shops, often enjoyed with a cup of coffee or tea.

Top 10 beaches in Mykonos

Enjoy the sea and the sun on our suggested top 10 beaches in Mykonos.
The position of each beach can be found on the map at the end of this guide.

1. Elia beach

If you're looking for a pristine, golden sandy beach with crystal-clear waters, Elia Beach is the perfect destination. Located just 8km from Mykonos Town, this idyllic stretch of coastline offers an unforgettable swimming experience, as well as a wealth of well-organized facilities and activities to cater to every visitor. Don't be surprised if you find yourself rubbing shoulders with celebrities, and be sure to have your camera ready to capture the memories. Elia Beach is also recognized as one of Mykonos' "gay-friendly" spots, featuring separate areas for gay and nudist visitors.

A Day at Elia Beach:
Upon arriving at Elia Beach, you'll be greeted by a vast expanse of soft, golden sand and inviting turquoise waters. Spend the day lounging on comfortable sunbeds beneath a shady umbrella, available for a cost of around €30 for a set of two sunbeds and an umbrella. Enjoy the

peaceful sound of waves lapping at the shore as you soak up the sun and immerse yourself in the beach's vibrant atmosphere.

Amenities and Activities:
Elia Beach boasts a range of well-organized facilities, ensuring that you have everything you need for a perfect day at the beach. Quench your thirst and satisfy your hunger at the beach's bars and restaurants, which offer a wide selection of food and drinks. Whether you're in the mood for a refreshing cocktail or a delicious meal, Elia Beach's dining options cater to every taste.

For those seeking more adventure, Elia Beach is an ideal location for water sports enthusiasts. The beach offers a variety of activities, including jet-skiing, windsurfing, and parasailing, providing an adrenaline rush for thrill-seekers. Alternatively, if you prefer a more leisurely pace, rent a paddleboard or take a leisurely swim in the calm, crystal-clear waters.

Gay-Friendly and Nudist Areas:
Elia Beach is well-known for its inclusive and welcoming atmosphere, with designated areas for both gay and nudist visitors. The beach's gay-friendly section is particularly popular, offering a lively and open-minded environment for members of the LGBTQ+ community to relax and socialize. The separate nudist area provides a space for those who prefer a more liberated beach experience, allowing visitors to sunbathe and swim au naturel in a judgement-free zone.

Getting to Elia Beach:
Elia Beach is easily accessible from Mykonos Town, located just 8km away. There are several transportation options available, including public buses, which run regularly from Mykonos Town, taxis, or car and scooter rentals. If you prefer a more scenic journey, consider taking a water taxi from Platis Gialos or Ornos Beach, which offers a unique and enjoyable way to reach Elia Beach.

2. Panormos beach

Nestled on the northern coast of Mykonos, Panormos Beach offers a serene and picturesque escape from the bustling island life. This tranquil, crescent-shaped beach boasts soft sands, clear azure waters, and a secluded atmosphere, making it an ideal destination for a relaxing beach getaway. The upscale beach club, Principote, elevates the Panormos Beach experience, providing visitors with luxurious amenities and exceptional services amidst the stunning natural beauty of the Mykonian coastline.

Panormos Beach: A Secluded Paradise

Panormos Beach's pristine sands and calm waters create the perfect setting for a peaceful day at the beach. The beach's remote location on the northern side of the island offers a more secluded and tranquil atmosphere compared to the busier southern beaches. Enjoy sunbathing, swimming, and taking in the breathtaking views of the surrounding hills and the sparkling Aegean Sea.

While Panormos Beach is less developed than other beaches on Mykonos, visitors can still find basic amenities such as sunbeds and umbrellas. For those seeking more privacy, the eastern end of the beach offers a quieter area where you can relax away from the crowd.

Principote: A Luxurious Beach Club Experience

Principote Beach Club elevates the Panormos Beach experience by providing visitors with a luxurious and stylish environment to enjoy the beach's natural beauty. The beach club boasts high-quality facilities, including comfortable sunbeds and umbrellas, elegant lounge areas, and chic decor that blends harmoniously with the surrounding landscape.

Indulge in the sophisticated culinary offerings at the Principote restaurant, which serves a delectable selection of Mediterranean and international dishes prepared by skilled chefs. Savor your meal in the elegant open-air dining area while taking in the magnificent views of Panormos Beach and the Aegean Sea.

The beach club also features a trendy bar where you can enjoy refreshing cocktails, premium spirits, and a carefully curated wine list. As the sun sets, the atmosphere at Principote transforms into a lively social scene, with DJ sets and live music creating the perfect soundtrack for an unforgettable Mykonian evening.

Getting to Panormos Beach and Principote
Panormos Beach is located approximately 7.5km from Mykonos Town, and the best way to reach it is by car or scooter rental due to limited public transportation options. If you prefer not to drive, you can also arrange for a taxi or private transfer to take you to the beach.

Sunbeds in Principote de Mykonos Beach Bar:
2 Sunbeds, umbrella and towels: 60€
2 Sunbeds, umbrella and towels (1st row at the beach): 90€

3. Kalo Livadi beach

At the southern part of Mykonos, between Elia and Kalafatis beaches, you may find one of the largest beaches of the island, Kalo Livadi. You can reach it either by using any land transport means or by the sea. Fully equipped with sunbeds, beach bars and taverns, this beach seems is ideal to offer you a relaxing and pleasant stay.

Altro Seaside Trattoria: 2 Sunbeds and umbrella: 35€

4. Agia Anna

If you want your piece of mind, a beach to chill out, Agia Anna is a good a option to go to. A quiet small beach, with crystal clear waters and not too many sunbeds. At Agia Anna, there is the Diving center where you can get lessons or participate in an underwater exploratory trip for advanced or beginners. Near the beach, you may find 'Nikolas tavern' which has homemade and traditional food. It is definitely worth to visit.

2 Sunbeds and umbrella: 30€- 40€ and 50€ (1st raw at the beach)

5. Agios Sostis

Agios Sostis, is one of the largest sandy, windy beaches of the island, ideal for wind surfing. Located at the north side of the island, it can only be reached by your own vehicle. You will not find any sunbeds or beach bars there, so do not forget to take some water and snacks with you. At the top of the hill, you may find 'Kiki's Tavern', where you can taste traditional specialties and grilled dishes (open during lunchtime only).

6. Platis Gialos

This beach, the longest of the island, attract lots of families and watersports lovers, due to its endless golden shore, the plenty of facilities and its ease access. It is located at the south side of Mykonos, only 4,5km from the town. Platis Gialos is perfect for swimming, fishing and lots of aquatic activities. From this beach, start the boats that make routes to other south beaches such as Paradise and Super Paradise.

Branco Mykonos: 2 Sunbeds and umbrella (1st row): 80€, 2 Sunbeds and umbrella (2nd and 3rd row): 60€

7. Super Paradise

This beach is located in a blue bay with wonderful view, only 6 km distance southwest from Mykonos town. Swim at the amazing crystal clear sea, sunbathe or enjoy your cocktail and dance at the allday parties of the beach bars. Lots of young people and VIPs from allover the world visit this place, in order to have fun and relax. During the day, the beach is a great spot for sunbathers, but in the late afternoon the party begins. The parties there last till morning and offer an unforgettable experience of summer relaxation and joy to everyone.

2 Sunbeds and umbrella(1st row): 40€
2 Sunbeds and umbrella (2nd and 3rd row): 30€ and 25€

8. Paradise

Next to the Super Paradise, 6km from the town, the Paradise beach is very popular for its parties, the watersports and the well-organized beach bars. Tropicana beach bar, the most popular Paradise beach bar, is one of the best party spots allover world. Late in the afternoon the music is getting louder and the party starts till early in the morning. Very often boats depart from the beach and take the visitors to the Super Paradise.

Mykonos Nightlife Guide

Mykonos is a top destination for active and crazy nightlife, attracting many young people from all over the world every year. In our Mykonos nightlife guide you will discover amazing beaches, elegant nightclubs and beach bars with international DJs that party at all hours of the day and night: Mykonos is definitely the greatest competitor of Ibiza.

Have a look below to discover the best places to party in Mykonos during the day or night.

CAVO PARADISO

Cavo Paradiso is Mykonos' premier out-of-town club and deserves a premium position in our Mykonos nightlife guide. With a huge open-air dancefloor, Cavo Paradiso invites every year the most popular DJs from around the world and one of its best selling points is how it manages to incorporate the island's natural beauty with a superb design. For tickets, the best way is via promoters that sell tickets on beaches and bus stations with discounts

Website: **cavoparadiso.gr**| Opening times: 11.30pm - 7am

54

A chic addition to Mykonos nightlife scene, @54 is a lounge bar and dance club that attracts a varied clientele. The sunset view terrace is the perfect place to snap a great picture while enjoying old school disco music perfectly mixed with house. Live performances on Wednesdays and Saturday with drinks reasonably priced.

facebook.com/at54Club/ | Opening times: 9pm - 4am

BABYLON

With a predominantly gay clientele with funny themed nights and drag shows, Babylon gives its best after midnight. Mainstream music, techno and oldies take the clientele through the night until early morning. Décor and seaside location complete the setting for a great night out. Cocktails prices are average and they offer one of the best Cosmopolitan in town

Website:https://www.facebook.com/babylonmyk/ | Opening times: 7.30pm - 6am

SKANDINAVIAN BAR AND CLUB

Perfect combination of reasonably priced amazing cocktails, open-air dance floor and patio area, Skandinavian Bar & Club hosted the best nights for youngsters for almost 40 years. This club gets busy after midnight so better not get there too early to avoid spending your night talking only to the staff before the actual party starts.

Website:https://www.skandinavianbar.com/ | Opening times: 8pm - 6am

ASTRA

Astra is the place to go for whatever type of night you are after. Being somewhat of a hybrid between a lounge bar and a nightclub, you can experience a more casual atmosphere in the evening and an authentic club during the night. Being designed by Minas, a world renowned jeweler, it's best feature is the fibreoptic ceiling that mimics the night sky of the northern hemisphere and pulses in time to the music

Website:http://www.astra-mykonos.com/Astra.html| Opening times: 8pm - 8am

SUPER PARADISE BEACH CLUB

Mykonos party scene must include the Super Paradise Beach Club with parties that start from the afternoon and last until early morning. Super Paradise has made its name a synonym to Party in Mykonos and being packed with clubbers, jet-setters, models and VIPs, do not get surprised if you spot a celebrity among the crowd or dancing next to you.

https://www.superparadise.com.gr

MONTPARNASSE – THE PIANO BAR

For a relaxed but still good night out, this is the place to go. Ideal for a romantic night out, The Piano Bar offers some of the best cocktails on the island. As the time goes by, after sunset the experience is enriched by cabaret entertainment with amazing views at the back of the piano bar, where the windows open up and you are in an area over the sea! It's great with the fresh breeze blowing through the bar.

Website:http://www.thepianobar.com/ | Opening times: 7pm - 3am

QUEEN OF MYKONOS

A glamorous name for a glamorous champagne and cocktail bar which doesn't make it the best option price-wise. Open from early in the morning and located at the centre of Chora, it's the perfect bar to enjoy a drink in a relaxed and fun atmosphere. DJs are on stage during the night but Queen of Mykonos is best as a warm-up before other super clubs in town

Website:https://queenofmykonos.gr/ | Opening times: 8pm - 5am

180° SUNSET BAR

The breathtaking view over Mykonos from Castle Panigirakis can hardly be beaten. A pure joy for senses with incredible cocktails and chillout music, it is ideal for a relaxing evening but make sure you have a camera with you to snap some photos of the sunset but seats with view need advance reservation and are subject to a fee.

Website: http://mykonoscastle.eu/180-sunset-bar/

SCORPIOS

Quite new in the scene, Scorpios was born in 2015 as a modern reimagining of ancient social rites and island ritual based on the five pillars of food, healing, design, art and music. Perfect as start of a night out as events generally wrap up at midnight. Sundays are the busiest day as it feels like the whole island gathers at Scorpios.

Website:https://www.scorpiosmykonos.com/
Opening times: 11am - 1am

ALLEY COCKTAIL BAR

Enjoy the ultimate cocktail experience at Alley, specialized in handcrafted cocktails made with elixirs, syrups and infusion from garden herbs and spices. Whilst accommodating your order, the bartender will also discuss how to best enjoy your drink with fresh fruits, flavors and spirits. Acid jazz, rare grooves, funk, jazz and reggae will be your soundtrack for the night.

Website:http://www.alleybar-mykonos.com/
Opening times: 8.30pm - 3am

TROPICANA BEACH BAR & RESTAURANT

Welcome to one of the Sexiest Beach Bar in the world according to the Travel Channel for 2012. Tropicana attracts young people in swimwear to party from the afternoon until 5am. Refreshing drinks and fanciful cocktails will cool people down in the heat of summer and keep partygoers in high spirit. Drinks are reasonably priced and so is the food.

Website: https://www.tropicanamykonos.com/

MONI

The club was founded by a diverse group of people from all over the world who have been coming to the island every summer for over 25 years. Experts on Mykonos' nightlife, they have created a place where both island regulars and first-timers, will feel at home. With international djs, VIP catering and master mixologists, a night at Moni promised to be an unforgettable and different experience as it is not easy to get in but its definitely worth to give it a try as the atmosphere inside will take you to another level!

Website:http://www.monimykonos.com/
Opening times: 12noon - 6.30am

VOID

Void is the club for everyone. Split in 3 levels with dancefloors, tables and booths, this club is a very recent addition to Mykonos nightlife. Deep house and techno are the soundtrack of VOID's nights

Website:https://www.void-mykonos.com/
Opening times: 11pm - 8am

SEMELI

Even though it can't compete in dimensions with other big clubs on the islands, music is key at Semeli, offering a great variety form hip hop to latin and house. But don't be fooled! Great drink deals (2-4-1) make the Semeli a good shout for a night out in Mykonos

Website:http://semelithebar.gr/new/
Opening times: 24h

CINE MANTO

Clubbing is life for some but not for all. Cine Manto is an open-air cinema playing movies in original language and acts as a shelter from the sometimes bustled and energetic lifestyle of Mykonos. Two movies are played every day and it is also possible to buy a Members Card if this is how you prefer to spend your nights in Mykonos. Cine Manto is one of the best places to enjoy Greek food at affordable prices

Website: http://www.cinemanto.gr/

BUDDHA BAR BEACH

Buddha Bar Beach hosts an array of celebrity DJ'S throughout the summer, creating unique events, amidst gatherings of beautiful people, who are bringing to Mykonos a unique ever-evolving lifestyle experience. Buddha Bar is a very exclusive experience that comes with high prices for food and drinks

91

Website:https://www.buddhabarbeachmykonos.gr/
Opening times: 7pm - 1am

CAPRICE OF MYKONOS

Caprice is an easy add to our Mykonos nightlife guide. Acclaimed by Newsweek as one of the 10 best bars worldwide and cherished by international celebrities, Caprice Bar is the perfect party destination with an incredible ambience and entertainment. Cocktails range between 15-19€

Website:http://capriceofmykonos.com/
Opening times: 6.30pm - 5am

LOLA BAR

Laid back music and great cocktails enjoyed in an elegant environment. This is Lola, in the heart of Mykonos Town. Cozy ambience, friendly staff and open-minded guests will make you feel comfortable and come back more and more.

Website:https://www.facebook.com/pages/category/Bar/LOLA-MYKONOS-90788959790/
Opening times: 12.30am - 3pm / 8pm - 12am

JACKIE O' BEACH CLUB AND RESTAURANT

With a 150 seat restaurant, large open bar, pool, jacuzzi and private lounge areas, its own church for ceremonies, the new Jackie O'

Beach Club is the latest hot meeting point of the island. High quality, excellent service and magnificent views will make you fall in love at once with this place. Might not be the cheapest option in Mykonos but the quality of cocktail will make you forget few euros more.

Website:https://www.jackieomykonos.com/
Opening times: 9am - 1 am

Top Things to Do in Mykonos in 3 Days

If you are planning to visit Mykonos for a three-day trip, you can enjoy a vibrant nightlife, breathtaking beaches, and stunning scenery. To make the most of your stay, here's a rundown of the top 10 things you can do on the island.

#1 Visit Caprice Bar: A must see in Mykonos, in the last 30 years!

Caprice bar is certainly the most famous bar of Mykonos. It is located on the sea, and you can enjoy great margaritas, happy people and great music, almost all time of the day. It hosts many great parties in the night, so don't forget to visit it at least once while you stay at Mykonos.

The facts about Mykonos, say that this island was home to only a few poor inhabitants 40 years ago,. Fishermen mainly and people raising goats and doing a little occasional commerce with the mainland of Greece. All of this changes once Mykonos started to become mainstream in the global jet set groups. And Caprice was their first choice for a meeting in the night. A lot of crazy nights have taken place here.

Keep in mind that as of a few years ago, due to a legal dispute between the owners of the place, **the name has to be changed**. But everybody in the island still refers to the bar as "Caprice," so just ask anyone to find your way there.

At the moment, Caprice is unfortunately closed due to this legal dispute and is under restoration from the new owner. So, just head there and have a table in a coffee shop next to it, in the area that is called "Little Venice." It is equally amazing, although the nights in Mykonos will not be the same until Caprice re-opens again.

The best time to go to Caprice would be either in the morning for a coffee (try **Freddo Espresso** or **Freddo Cappuccino** coffee), or in the evening, after 23:00 pm.

Here is the **view** you will enjoy from Caprice bar:

View from Caprice Bar in Mykonos to the Little Venice Area

#2 Go to Paraga Beach

Paraga beach, located a few kilometers away from Mykonos town, is a popular spot for tourists looking to soak up some sun and have some fun. It boasts a fantastic beach and a lively beach bar that attracts a lot of young people after 5 PM. To secure your spot, it's recommended to arrive early in the morning, around 10:00 am, to rent an umbrella and sunbed set. These cost around 30 Euros, but they are definitely worth it. You can also order drinks and coffees from the beach bar, which is conveniently located right on the beach.

If you're planning on visiting Paraga beach, there are a few things to keep in mind. The Kahlua Beach Bar is located in the middle of the beach and is one of the two most upscale beach bars in Mykonos, the other being the beach bar at Nammos restaurant in Psarou Beach. However, be aware that many famous customers have already reserved umbrella sets here, and there is a kind of "face control" at this beach bar. If you're alone and look like you might not be able to afford it, the "umbrella-sets manager" may politely tell you that everything is booked at the moment. Additionally, it can be quite expensive to rent an umbrella set at Kahlua Bar, costing 30 euros for two sunbeds and one umbrella. However, the sunbeds are luxurious and come with two towels.

If you want to save some money, there is another shop next to Kahlua Bar that rents umbrella sets. Here, an umbrella set for two costs 25 Euros if you're in the first line, just in front of the sea, and 20 Euros if you choose an umbrella set further back (3rd-4th line). A Freddo Espresso coffee costs 4.5 Euros, so for two people, you would pay a total of 25E + 9E = 34 Euros for an umbrella set and two coffees. A large 1-liter bottle of water costs 1.5 Euros.

No matter where you get your umbrella set from, you'll be able to enjoy the music from Kahlua beach bar, which plays lounge music until 5:00 pm and then switches to party music for 3-4 hours. The bar often hosts great parties, especially in August, so there is a lot of fun to be had in the afternoon. Paraga beach offers a great experience from 10:00 am until 9:00 pm, with the option to grab lunch at a taverna on the beach or at Kahlua Bar. Afterward, you can party until 9:00 pm, and then head back to Mykonos town for some rest or to continue exploring the nightlife.

Finally, if you're looking for other popular beaches in Mykonos, Platis Gialos Beach, Psarou Beach, Paradise and Super Paradise Beach, Panormos Beach, Elia Beach, and Agios Stefanos beach are also worth checking out.

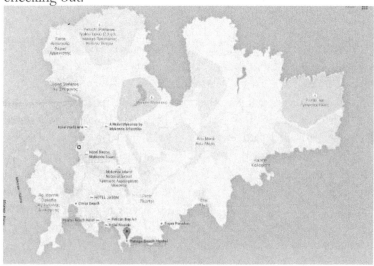

#3 Go to Super Paradise Beach

A Party at Super Paradise Beach in Mykonos

Super Paradise Beach, located a little far from the main town of Mykonos, is a huge beach with white sand and crystal-clear water, and is home to some of the craziest beach parties on the island. Along with Paradise Beach, known for its Tropicana beach bar, Super Paradise Beach is considered to be one of the liveliest and most exciting beaches in Mykonos.

However, be careful not to confuse the two beaches with similar names in Mykonos. Super Paradise Beach is the place to be for a wild beach party and is not as posh as other beaches like Psarou and Paraga. Despite the party scene, there is also a food spot on the beach where you can grab a quick lunch.

While it may not be for everyone, Super Paradise Beach is an experience you don't want to miss on your first visit to Mykonos. If you prefer a quieter time, head towards the east side of the beach where the music is less loud and there are no beach bars.

Check out the Super Paradise Beach Facebook page at https://www.facebook.com/superparadisebeachmykonos to get a feel for the vibe.

#4 Have a walk in Matoyiannia – the old town or "Chora of Mykonos." One of the main Mykonos attractions.

The old town of Mykonos is full of small white houses and romantic streets with fabulous flowers, while it hosts several bars and restaurants. You will find yourself strolling around for many hours in this magnificent area.

#5 Rent a Scooter and visit Kalo Livadi

Kalo Livadi beach may not be as popular as other beaches in Mykonos, but it is a hidden gem that the locals love. This serene beach offers visitors a peaceful retreat away from the crowds. The beach itself is stunning, with crystal clear waters and golden sands.

The beach bar on Kalo Livadi beach is also a highlight, serving refreshing drinks and delicious snacks. It's the perfect spot to unwind and enjoy the laid-back atmosphere of the beach. If you're looking for a peaceful and relaxing day on the beach, Kalo Livadi is the perfect spot.

#6 Have lunch at Kiki's Restaurant

Kiki's restaurant, located in Agios Sostis Village in Mykonos, is widely regarded as one of the best restaurants on the island. The menu features a variety of delicious dishes, including spaghetti with seafood, lobster, shrimp, and excellent Greek fish. However, due to its popularity, the restaurant does not accept reservations, so it is common to find a long line of people waiting to get a table. Typically, there are up to 20 people waiting in line, and the wait can range from 15 to 30 minutes. However, the owner provides guests with complimentary rose wine and water, and the waiting area offers stunning views of the small, non-touristy beach of Agios Sostis. The wait is well worth it, as Kiki's offers a truly unforgettable dining experience.

If you want to sample some of the best food in Mykonos, including delicious seafood spaghetti, lobsters, shrimps, and Greek fish, Kiki's restaurant is a must-visit. Located in the quaint Agios Sostis village, the restaurant is quite small, and they don't take reservations, so be prepared to wait. However, the stunning views of the non-touristy Agios Sostis beach, coupled with complimentary rose wine and water, make the wait bearable. You can even check out this video of the restaurant's interior: https://www.youtube.com/watch?v=CPvRDsQKMtY

Kiki's restaurant closes at 7 pm, and their prices are around 25 euros per person for a main course, two small dishes, and a couple of beers. While it's not cheap, you'll quickly learn that eating well on Mykonos can be pricey. One dish worth trying is the huge pork chop, which costs 17 euros and can easily satisfy your hunger.

For a perfect day out, head to either Agios Sostis beach or Panormos beach for a swim and then make your way to Kiki's for dinner around 4:30 pm. Agios Sostis beach doesn't have any umbrellas or beach bars, so make sure to bring your sun protection. Panormos beach, on the other hand, boasts an excellent beach bar and umbrella sets.

The Agios Sostis Beach in Mykonos

#7 Clubbing at Cavo Paradiso

An evening party at Cavo Paradiso

Cavo Paradiso, situated 10 km away from Mykonos town, is one of the most renowned summer clubs in Europe, sharing the top 3 with the ones located in Ibiza. The club hosts parties with world-class DJs like Tiesto. To make the most of your visit, we recommend going there after 1:00 AM and staying until the morning to catch the sunrise while enjoying breakfast after a night of non-stop partying. However, we should mention that this is mostly a club for people in their 20s, but of course, anyone who feels young and wild is always welcome! If you're curious about the events happening this summer at Cavo Paradiso, visit their website at http://cavoparadiso.gr/events/.

#8 Eat a Souvlaki

Souvlaki is the most popular street food of Greece, and everyone enjoys eating it. You can try it at several spots in the old town of Mykonos. Ask for "tzatziki" to be included in your "pita" with "souvlaki." Tzatziki is a famous Greek yogurt sauce with garlic and cucumber that you will love forever!

#9 Treat yourself at Nammos Restaurant and Psarrou Beach. One of the coolest things to do in Mykonos (and expensive ones..)

Dean and Dan from Dsquared, **on a beach catwalk at Nammos Beach Bar**

Psarou beach is a popular spot among the wealthy visitors of Mykonos, with the chance to see and be seen. However, it can be quite expensive. If you plan to visit, it's recommended to arrive early in the morning to secure a good spot on the beach and enjoy the crystal-clear waters. In the afternoon, you can treat yourself to a meal at Nammos restaurant, which is conveniently located on the beach.

To get to Psarou beach, which is located 4 km from Mykonos town, it's better to avoid driving as parking can be a challenge. Instead, you can park your car on the hill and walk down for about 300 meters. Once you arrive at Psarou beach, you'll find a well-protected area that is sheltered from the winds, unlike other beaches on the island. This makes it a great destination if you want to avoid battling the sand during windy days.

It's worth noting that many impressive yachts can be spotted at Psarou beach, as many of their owners come to enjoy the luxurious life and amenities provided by Nammos beach bar and restaurant. If you're looking for a glimpse of the high-end lifestyle on Mykonos, Psarou beach is definitely worth a visit. You can also watch this short video to get a better sense of the beach: https://www.youtube.com/watch?v=XiPbkkRBScI

Psarou beach is divided into three sections. The first section is owned by Nammos restaurant and beach bar, and it is the most expensive

one. In contrast, the second section, located in the middle of the beach, is owned by a cheap and disorganized snack bar. The third section belongs to a 5-star hotel situated on the beach.

Take a look at this picture featuring the famous sunbeds of Nammos restaurant. In the background of the photo, you can see the expensive "Riva" boat of the owner of Nammos, which costs around 1.2 million Euros. This boat is used to transfer the wealthy and famous customers from their yachts to the beach bar.

The sunbeds of Nammos Restaurant in Psarou Beach

The Nammos restaurant's section of Psarrou Beach is the priciest, with a set of two sunbeds and an umbrella costing a whopping 80 Euros. Meanwhile, the neighboring snack bar offers the same set of umbrellas for a more reasonable 25 Euros. This makes it the "Cheap Side of Psarou," as seen in the photo below featuring their simple sunbeds and umbrellas.

This kind of Sunbeds cost 25 Euros per set to rent for the day- The low-cost side of Psarou Beach

And here is the view from the "cheap side" of Psarou beach. Yes, you are swimming in the same waters with your wealthy neighbors!

Sunbeds in Psarou Beach - in front of the Snack Bar - next to Nammos Restaurant

#10 Clubbing at Lakka club (ex-Space Club)

Lakka club, owned by Foo Club Company, is situated in the heart of Mykonos town and is a convenient alternative to Cavo Paradiso for party lovers. It hosts various exciting parties and is a must-visit spot while in Mykonos. The club used to be known as "Space Club" for many years and is recognized by both names by the locals. It is recommended for those under 30 who are seeking a fun night out. You can check out Lakka club's Facebook page for some sneak peeks into their events:

https://www.facebook.com/FOU-CLUB-Mykonos-1383618725301389/

#11: Treat Yourself to a Luxurious Hotel Stay in Mykonos

Indulge in a once-in-a-lifetime experience and book a stay at one of Mykonos' luxurious hotels, even if it's just for one night. You will be treated like royalty and get to mingle with top artists and fashion designers, such as Armani. You can enjoy spectacular views of the island and be pampered with unparalleled service.

One of the most sought-after hotels in Mykonos is Cavo Tagoo, where Armani is a frequent guest. However, it may be considered quite pricey by some. You can find all the juicy stories of the rich and famous who have stayed at Cavo Tagoo by searching "Cavo Tagoo" on Google News. The hotel offers stunning views of Mykonos town and the

Aegean Sea, but there is no beach in front of the property, and you will have to travel elsewhere to swim, such as Agios Stefanos beach, which is 1.5 km away.

or stay at Mykonos Princess hotel at Agios Stefanos village, just a couple of km away from Mykonos town.

Another great hotel is a new entry, which has become the talk of the town and is called "Rocabella": **Click Here** to See the Rocabella Mykonos Hotel. It's located at Agios Stefanos village, which is 2kms outside of Mykonos.

#12. Make a Yacht Cruise to Delos and Rhenia Islands

Delos island is close to Mykonos, and it is a great archaeological island, while Rhenia Islands is an uninhabited island with crystal clear waters. The tour lasts 8 hours, costs around 90 euros per person and you can book it here.

The Strip of Sea that you see in this photo separates the two islands of Delos and Rhenia

You can also book the same tour, without Delos, if you just prefer to swim in the perfect blue waters of Rhenia islands. This trip takes 7 hours and costs 75 euros per person, while you can book it **here**.

Souvenirs to bring back home:

In Mykonos, you can find many shops where you can buy souvenirs, golden jewelry, textiles, magnets, postcards, etc. There also many Greek and international designer brand stores. You can find a list of souvenir and other shops **here**.

Top 3 places to watch the sunset in Mykonos

Mykonos is a beautiful island in Greece, well-known for its breathtaking sunsets that draw crowds of tourists every evening. If you want to witness the spectacular colors of the sunset in Mykonos, here are the top three places you should consider visiting:

1. **Little Venice, Mykonos Town:** Located in the heart of Mykonos Town, Little Venice is a picturesque neighborhood that offers a stunning view of the sunset. The colorful buildings perched on the edge of the sea create a magical atmosphere that is perfect for romantic walks and sunset watching.
2. **Armenistis Lighthouse:** Situated on the northern tip of Mykonos, the Armenistis Lighthouse offers a panoramic view of the Aegean Sea and the surrounding islands. This historic lighthouse is a popular spot for tourists and locals alike, who gather here to watch the sunset while enjoying the peaceful scenery.
3. **Windmills:** The iconic windmills of Mykonos are not only a symbol of the island but also a great spot to watch the sunset.

Located on a hill overlooking the sea, the windmills provide a stunning backdrop for the colorful sky as the sun sets behind the horizon.

Whether you prefer a lively atmosphere or a more serene setting, these three locations offer the perfect spots to catch the sunset in Mykonos. Don't forget to bring your camera and capture the moment to cherish forever.

View the related map online **here**

Daily excursions and activities

Mykonos, apart from its gorgeous beaches, lively nightlife and delicious food, also offers a variety of day trips and excursions to its visitors. Here are some of the best options to explore the island and its surroundings:

Delos Island Tour: Delos Island is a UNESCO World Heritage Site and one of the most important archaeological sites in Greece. The island is located just a few kilometers from Mykonos and can be reached by boat. A guided tour of the ancient ruins will take you back in time to the birthplace of Apollo and Artemis, with highlights such as the Terrace of the Lions, the House of Dionysus and the Archaeological Museum of Delos. -Delos tour

Island hopping: Mykonos is part of the Cyclades island group, and many other beautiful islands are easily accessible by ferry. You can take a day trip to nearby islands such as Tinos, Syros or Paros, and explore their unique culture, history and stunning landscapes.

Jeep Safari: For the adventurous types, a jeep safari around the island is a thrilling way to discover Mykonos' hidden gems, such as secluded beaches, charming villages and breathtaking views. A knowledgeable guide will take you off the beaten path and show you a different side of the island.

-Link to a Jeep safari activity

Mykonos Wine Tasting: Mykonos has a long tradition of winemaking, and a visit to one of its local wineries is a great way to experience the island's wine culture. You can taste a variety of wines made from indigenous grape varieties, such as Assyrtiko and Mandilaria, and learn about the winemaking process from the experts.

Wine tasting tour at Vioma farm

Horseback Riding: A horseback riding tour is an excellent way to see the island's countryside and beaches. Experienced guides will take you on a scenic route, passing through lush vegetation, vineyards and sandy shores. It's a unique and unforgettable way to experience Mykonos.

Sunset Cruise: Mykonos has some of the most beautiful sunsets in Greece, and a sunset cruise is a romantic and relaxing way to end your day. You can enjoy a refreshing drink and admire the stunning colors of the sunset over the Aegean Sea, while cruising around the island's coastline.:

Link to a **South coastline cruise**

Overall, Mykonos has plenty to offer in terms of day trips and excursions, catering to all tastes and preferences. Whether you're interested in history, nature, adventure or relaxation, you'll find something that suits you.

Mykonos is not just about partying and lounging on the beach. There are also plenty of thrilling activities to try out, such as scuba diving, windsurfing, and kite surfing.

Scuba diving is a great way to explore the island's underwater world. There are several dive centers on the island that offer courses for all levels, from beginners to experienced divers. Some of the popular dive sites include the Delos Island wrecks, the Paradise Reef, and the Kalo Livadi Wall. You'll get to see colorful marine life, underwater caves, and stunning rock formations.

Link to A suggested Scuba diving activity

Windsurfing and **kite surfing** are perfect for those who love water sports. Mykonos is a windy island, and its beaches are ideal for windsurfing and kite surfing. The most popular spots for these activities are Korfos Beach, Ftelia Beach, and Kalafatis Beach. There are also windsurfing and kite surfing schools where you can take lessons or rent equipment.

Link to Windsurfing and Kite surfing activity.

115

A 3-Day Itinerary with the Best Things to Do in Mykonos

If you have three days to spend in this stunning Greek island, you have enough time to explore some of the best things it has to offer. From enjoying the crystal-clear waters of its beaches to experiencing the vibrant nightlife, Mykonos has something for everyone. In this itinerary, we have gathered the top activities and sights that you should not miss during your visit, to help you make the most out of your time on the island. So, let's get started on this exciting journey!

1st Day In Mykonos - Itinerary

9:00 AM – Arrival at Mykonos Airport
Arrive at Mykonos International Airport, which is located 4km from the town center.

9:30 AM – Airport to Mykonos Chora
Take the bus to the town center, hail a taxi directly to your hotel, rent a car, or arrange for your hotel's staff to pick you up. Check-in to your room.
Cost: 1.6 euros (bus), around 15 euros (taxi)

10:00 AM – Visit Paraportiani and a Museum
After settling in, head to the town to visit the Archaeological Museum and Paraportiani church.
The Archaeological Museum of Mykonos showcases the island's history from the prehistoric to the Hellenistic era. Although small, it is an interesting museum for history enthusiasts.
Cost: 2 euros

Paraportiani church, dedicated to Holy Mary, is actually a cluster of five churches that were joined over the years. The temple dates back to 1425 and is a famous sight. The name Paraportiani means "at the door side," as the church was originally located near the entrance of the Medieval castle of the town, which was destroyed later on.

Cost: free

12:30 PM – Beach Time at Platis Gialos
Make your way to Platis Gialos Beach.
Swimming and sunbathing are a must-do in Mykonos! For today, we recommend visiting Platis Gialos beach, which is just a 15-minute drive (5 km) from the town center.
View TOP 10+1 beaches.

14:00 - Lunch at Blue Myth Restaurant
Address: Petinos hotels, Platis Gialos, **Tel:** 2289 022127

15:00 – Beach Time
Choose another beach located in the south to spend your day swimming and sunbathing. You can refer to the list of the top 10 beaches provided below to make your selection.

18:30 – Dinner at Yialo Yialo
Head back to Platis Gialos and have dinner at Yialo Yialo tavern. After your meal, head back to the hotel.
Address: Platis Gialos, Mykonos, **Tel:** 2289 078916

20:00 – A walk around Matoyianni, Mykonos Chora
Take a break and stroll around the charming cobblestoned streets of the town by night. Explore the vibrant Matoyianni Street, picturesque Little Venice, and the iconic windmills. Mykonos nights are perfect for late-night revelries! If you fancy a drink or a beer, there are plenty of bars and clubs to choose from. Check out our recommended spots on the map for tonight's adventures.

Below, you will find maps that correspond to all the recommended activities for your first day in Mykonos. These maps are available on Google Maps, allowing you to easily zoom in and out and access them on your tablet or smartphone while in Mykonos.

Click here to view the map online or visit bit.ly/mykonos1stday or scan the QR code below if you are an offline reader.

Discovering Mykonos' Ancient Treasures: A Visit to the Archaeological Museum of Mykonos

photo by www.gtp.gr

The Archaeological Museum of Mykonos is a must-visit destination for travelers interested in exploring the island's rich history and ancient past. Established in 1902, the museum is located in Mykonos Town and houses an impressive collection of artifacts unearthed from various archaeological sites across the island and its neighboring isles, including Delos and Rhenia. A visit to the Archaeological Museum offers a unique opportunity to gain insights into the ancient civilizations that once inhabited Mykonos and to appreciate the incredible artistic achievements of these bygone cultures.

Exhibits and Collections:
The Archaeological Museum of Mykonos showcases a diverse range of exhibits that cover various periods, from the Prehistoric to the Late Hellenistic era. These captivating displays provide a comprehensive overview of the island's ancient history and the daily lives of its inhabitants. Among the many fascinating exhibits, visitors will find:

1. Pottery Collection: Admire an extensive collection of pottery, including vases, amphorae, and kylixes, which span from the

119

Geometric period to the Hellenistic era. The intricate geometric designs and mythological scenes depicted on these artifacts provide valuable insights into the artistic trends and cultural beliefs of the time.

2. Grave Stelae: Explore a remarkable selection of grave stelae, funerary sculptures that marked the burial sites of Mykonos' ancient inhabitants. The inscriptions and imagery on these marble monuments offer a unique window into the customs and social structures of the period.

3. Sculptures: Marvel at the museum's impressive array of ancient sculptures, which includes statues, busts, and reliefs. These stunning works of art provide a fascinating glimpse into the artistic and aesthetic sensibilities of the ancient Mykonians.

4. Mosaics and Frescoes: Discover the intricate craftsmanship of the island's ancient artisans through beautifully preserved mosaics and frescoes, which adorned the floors and walls of the island's ancient structures.

5. Jewelry and Personal Items: Gain insights into the daily lives and personal adornments of Mykonos' ancient inhabitants through a captivating collection of jewelry, coins, and other personal items.

Practical Information:

The Archaeological Museum of Mykonos is situated in Mykonos Town, within walking distance from the old port. The museum is open year-round, with daily operating hours from 8:30 am to 3:30 pm, except for Tuesdays when the museum is closed. Admission fees apply, with reduced rates available for students, seniors, and groups. Guided tours can be arranged upon request.

Paraportiani Church: A Unique Architectural Marvel in Mykonos

Paraportiani Church, also known as Panagia Paraportiani, is one of the most iconic and photographed landmarks in Mykonos. Located in the Kastro neighborhood of Mykonos Town, this unique religious complex is a testament to the island's architectural heritage and serves as a symbol of Mykonian tradition. A visit to Paraportiani Church is a must for travelers who wish to explore the island's rich history and appreciate the beauty of its distinct architecture.

A Singular Architectural Ensemble:

What sets Paraportiani Church apart is its one-of-a-kind structure, which is composed of five individual churches that were built over a period of two centuries, between the 15th and 17th centuries. The churches are constructed in the traditional Cycladic style, featuring whitewashed walls, curved lines, and simple yet elegant forms. The asymmetrical arrangement of the churches creates a unique, harmonious blend of architectural elements that has captivated visitors and photographers for generations.

The Five Churches:

Paraportiani Church comprises four ground-level chapels and one upper-level church, each with its own distinct character and history:

1. Agios Efstathios: This central church is the largest of the five and serves as the main place of worship within the complex.

2. Agios Anargyros: Situated to the east of Agios Efstathios, this chapel is dedicated to Saint Anargyros, the patron saint of physicians.
3. Agios Sozon: Located to the north of Agios Efstathios, this chapel is dedicated to Saint Sozon, the protector of sailors.
4. Agia Anastasia: Found on the southern side of the complex, this chapel is dedicated to Saint Anastasia, the patron saint of weavers.
5. Panagia Paraportiani: The upper-level church, from which the complex takes its name, is dedicated to the Virgin Mary (Panagia). The name "Paraportiani" refers to its location near the side entrance (paraporti) of the medieval castle that once stood in the Kastro neighborhood.

Visiting Paraportiani Church:
While the church is not always open to the public, visitors are welcome to admire its exterior and enjoy the serene atmosphere that surrounds the complex. The church is easily accessible on foot from Mykonos Town, and its location near the old port offers stunning views of the sea.

Make sure to visit Paraportiani Church during different times of the day, as the sunlight creates a mesmerizing play of shadows on the whitewashed walls, enhancing the structure's unique beauty. Sunset, in particular, is a magical time to capture the enchanting glow that envelops the church.

09:30 - Take a tour of Delos island
Delos island is 2 km away from Mykonos (30-45' by small boat). It was of vital importance in the Ancient years, and it is considered a World Heritage Site. The whole island is an open-air museum. It is a place worth visiting, and it is a must for history and mythology lovers. Book a guided tour to Delos here

Cost: 50 euros | View ZoomTip 2.2

15:00 - Lunch at one of our 15 suggested restaurants in Mykonos town. If you plan to go to Agios Sostis beach, consider Kiki's tavern, which is just next to it.

15.30 – Enjoy some Beach Time
Choose one of the east beaches (Panormos, Agios Sostis or both!)
View Top 10 beaches in Mykonos

19:00 – Armenistis Lighthouse
Take the road to Armenistis Lighthouse. Enjoy the view and take some photos from the hill!

20:00 – Dinner at Captain's
Have dinner at Captain's restaurant in Mykonos town and return to your room, to take some rest and get ready for a night out!

Captain's Restaurant: Address: Mykonos Waterfront, **Tel.** 2289 023283

For tonight you can take a walk in the town for some bar hopping and continue partying until late midnight! There are too many night clubs and bars to choose from.

2nd Day in Mykonos – Map

Below you can get the maps that correspond to all the activities that we recommend for your second day in Mykonos. These maps are accessible in Google Maps format so that you can quickly zoom in/out, navigate and use them from your tablet or smartphone when you are in Mykonos.

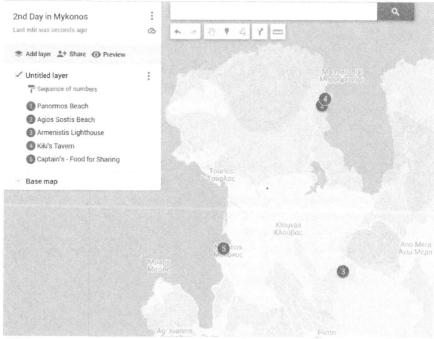

Click here to view the map online or visit bit.ly/mykonos2nd or scan the below QR code if you are an offline reader.

A Day Trip to Delos: Exploring the Birthplace of Apollo and Artemis

Delos, an UNESCO World Heritage Site, is a small yet historically significant island located just a short boat ride from Mykonos. As the mythical birthplace of the ancient Greek gods Apollo and Artemis, the island boasts a wealth of archaeological treasures and stunning ruins. A day trip to Delos offers an unforgettable journey through time, providing a unique opportunity to delve into the island's rich history and immerse yourself in the wonders of ancient Greece.

The Journey to Delos: Embark on your day trip to Delos by taking one of the regular boats that operate between Mykonos and Delos during the tourist season. The boat ride takes approximately 30 minutes, and the stunning views of the Aegean Sea make for a pleasant journey. Once you arrive at Delos, you'll be welcomed by a small harbor and a view of the archaeological site that awaits your exploration.

Key Historical Sites and Monuments: The archaeological site at Delos is vast and well-preserved, offering a wealth of ancient monuments and structures to explore. Some of the key sites to visit during your day trip include:

- The Sanctuary of Apollo: As the island's main religious center, this sanctuary was dedicated to Apollo, the god of light, music, and harmony. Here, you can discover the remains of three temples dedicated to Apollo, as well as several altars and the iconic Terrace of the Lions, featuring a row of marble lions that once guarded the sanctuary.
- The House of Dionysus: Named after the beautiful mosaic of Dionysus riding a panther found in this well-preserved private residence, the House of Dionysus offers a fascinating glimpse into the daily life of the island's wealthy inhabitants during the Hellenistic period.
- The House of Cleopatra: Located near the theater district, this opulent residence is named after the two statues of Cleopatra and Dioscourides, who once owned the house. Marvel at the intricate mosaics and the impressive architecture, which showcase the affluence of Delos during its heyday.
- The Theater: With a capacity of 5,500 spectators, the ancient theater of Delos hosted plays, musical performances, and competitions. Climb the steps to take in the magnificent view of the surrounding ruins and the Aegean Sea.
- The Archaeological Museum of Delos: Enhance your visit to Delos by exploring the museum, which houses a remarkable collection of artifacts unearthed during the excavations on the island. Highlights include statues, mosaics, and everyday items that provide a deeper understanding of the island's history and its inhabitants.

Tips for Your Day Trip:

Wear comfortable shoes and bring sunscreen, as you'll be walking extensively around the archaeological site, which has little shade.

Bring water and snacks, as options on the island are limited.

Allocate at least three to four hours to explore the island and fully appreciate its historical significance.

Consider hiring a licensed guide or joining a guided tour to gain deeper insights into the history and significance of the various monuments and structures.

Armenistis Lighthouse

Armenistis Lighthouse, also known as Faros Armenistis, is a historical lighthouse located on the northern tip of Mykonos. It was built in 1891 by the French company of Lighthouses and Beacons and was operated by French keepers until 1983. The lighthouse stands at a height of 19 meters and emits a white flash every 10 seconds that can be seen up to 18 nautical miles away. It was built to assist navigation and to prevent shipwrecks in the treacherous waters surrounding the island. The lighthouse itself is an impressive structure, with its white and red stripes and a cylindrical tower made of stone. It is considered one of the most important landmarks on the island and a popular spot for tourists to visit. The area around the lighthouse offers panoramic views of the Aegean Sea and the neighboring islands, making it a perfect place to watch the sunset.It is located in Fanari, which means lantern in Greek, 6.5 km (4.0 miles) from Chora

3d Day in Mykonos – Itinerary

8:30 – Visit a Gallery and a Museum Start your day by checking out from your hotel and heading towards the Agricultural Museum – Boni Mill, located in Mykonos Town. This iconic landmark offers a glimpse into the island's agricultural past. Although the museum may be closed, the stunning view of the city and the sea makes it worth a visit.
Next, explore Dio Horia, a contemporary art gallery featuring intriguing exhibitions that showcase the vibrant local and international art scene.
View ZoomTip 3.1

11:00 – Beach Time Head to the town's beach for some farewell swimming and sunbathing. Relax and enjoy the crystal-clear waters and warm sands before your departure.

14:30 – Lunch at Kastro's Restaurant Savor a delicious lunch at Kastro's restaurant, a charming eatery known for its traditional Greek cuisine and stunning views. Address: Agion Anargiron 1, Mykonos, tel. 2289 023072

15:30 – Aegean Maritime Museum Immerse yourself in the history of merchant shipping in the Aegean Sea area by visiting the Aegean Maritime Museum. The museum's interactive and "living" exhibitions provide a unique and informative experience.
View ZoomTip 3.1

17:00 – Leisurely Stroll and Shopping Before heading to the airport, take a leisurely stroll around Mykonos Town, explore its picturesque alleys, and browse the local shops for unique souvenirs and gifts to bring back home.

18:30 – Sunset Drinks Cap off your Mykonos adventure with a refreshing drink at one of the island's many bars or cafes, offering panoramic views of the sunset. Toast to your unforgettable trip and the memories you've made.

19:30 – Depart for the Airport Head to the airport, filled with memories of your incredible time in Mykonos, and begin your journey home or to your next destination.

3.1: Information on the Monuments

Unearthing Mykonos' Past: A Visit to the Agricultural Museum

The Agricultural Museum of Mykonos is a fascinating destination for travelers seeking to explore the island's rich agricultural history and traditional way of life. Located in Mykonos Town, close to the famous Windmills of Kato Mili, the museum occupies a beautifully restored 16th-century windmill known as the "Boni Windmill." This unique setting provides an ideal backdrop for visitors to immerse themselves in the island's rural past and gain an appreciation for the hard work and ingenuity of the local farmers who shaped Mykonos' cultural heritage.
Exhibits and Collections: The Agricultural Museum showcases a diverse range of exhibits that highlight various aspects of traditional farming practices, tools, and techniques. These displays offer a valuable insight into the lives and daily routines of Mykonian farmers throughout history. Among the many intriguing exhibits, visitors will find:

1. Farming Implements: Explore a captivating collection of agricultural tools and machinery, including plows, threshing

machines, and winnowing fans, used by Mykonian farmers to cultivate and harvest their crops.

2. Windmill Machinery: Delve into the inner workings of the historic Boni Windmill, which has been meticulously preserved to showcase the ingenious mechanisms used to harness the power of the wind for milling grain.

3. Traditional Pottery: Admire an assortment of handcrafted pottery, including storage jars and other containers, which played a vital role in preserving food and beverages for the local population.

4. Local Produce: Gain an appreciation for the island's abundant natural resources with displays featuring traditional Mykonian products, such as olive oil, wine, and honey, which continue to be vital components of the local economy.

5. Period Photographs: Take a step back in time with an evocative collection of photographs, capturing the daily lives of Mykonian farmers and their families as they toiled the land and tended to their animals.

Outdoor Exhibits: The Agricultural Museum's idyllic surroundings provide a fitting setting for several engaging outdoor exhibits, which include:

1. Traditional Animal Shelters: Explore the "Mitato," a circular stone structure used by farmers to shelter their livestock, particularly goats and sheep, during the harsh winter months.

2. Gardens and Crops: Wander through the museum's well-tended gardens, which showcase a variety of indigenous plants, herbs, and crops that have sustained the people of Mykonos for centuries.

Practical Information: The Agricultural Museum is situated in Mykonos Town, a short walk from the iconic windmills of Kato Mili. The museum is open from May to October, with daily operating hours from 4:00 pm to 8:00 pm. Admission is free, but donations are appreciated to help maintain the site and its exhibits.

Dio Horia gallery

Dio Horia is an art platform & gallery for contemporary art and culture that was inaugurated in 2015. Through a vibrant program of exhibitions, residencies, events, publications and pop-up bookshops, Dio Horia gallery stimulates debate, experimentation, creativity and knowledge exchange with the audience. Founded by Marina Vranopoulou, Dio Horia gallery supports artists in the development and exhibition of their work. Also, Dio Horia gallery encourages a dialogue between the local and global art scene, promoting Greek and international art to a wider audience.

Dio Horia gallery strives to be at the forefront of cultural experimentation both in Greece and the world beyond, by presenting important solo and group shows by established artists. At the same time, a generation of young artists will take part in exhibitions and residencies. Dio Horia engages in collaborative projects developed as a result of associations with artists, curators, non-profit organizations and cultural carriers. These fall into categories ranging from social, cultural and literary studies to music and performing arts. Through these collaborations, Dio Horia plays host to diverse viewpoints and aesthetics.

The name Dio Horia is inspired by the book by Greek architect Aris Konstantinidis entitled Dio Horia from Mykonos, where the phrase "Dio Horia" means both "two spaces" and "two villages." Besides its primary location in Mykonos, Dio Horia gallery's activities move nomadically from one place to another, to study each area's different social aspects, and therefore become the driving force behind the artistic practice. These sites are as popular as Mykonos to the non-art initiated public, and present, again like Mykonos, an engaging and dynamic social situation.

Visit the Website

Aegean Maritime Museum

Nestled in the heart of the iconic island of Mykonos, the Aegean Maritime Museum offers an enthralling experience for travelers seeking a deeper understanding of the region's rich maritime history. Established in 1983 by George M. Drakopoulos, this private, non-profit institution aims to preserve and showcase the maritime heritage of the Aegean Sea. Housed within a beautiful, traditional Cycladic building in the bustling area of Mykonos Town, the museum is a must-visit destination for history buffs, maritime enthusiasts, and inquisitive travelers alike.

Exhibits and Collections: The Aegean Maritime Museum boasts an impressive array of exhibits and collections that trace the evolution of maritime trade, shipping, and nautical techniques in the Aegean Sea. From the prehistoric era to the present day, the museum's displays offer a comprehensive insight into the region's naval development. Among the various exhibits, visitors will find:

1. Ship Models: Admire the intricate craftsmanship of ship models representing ancient, medieval, and modern vessels. These models provide a fascinating visual representation of the evolution of ship design and construction throughout the ages.

2. Nautical Instruments: Discover a collection of nautical instruments, including antique compasses, astrolabes, and sextants,

133

that were essential tools for sailors navigating the treacherous waters of the Aegean Sea.

3. Maps and Charts: Uncover the mysteries of the sea with a stunning assortment of maps and charts that depict the Aegean region's changing geographical and political landscape over the centuries.

4. Maritime Art: Delight in the museum's selection of maritime-themed paintings, sculptures, and other artwork, which capture the essence of life at sea and the culture of the islands.

5. Lighthouse Collection: The museum houses a unique collection of lighthouse replicas from around the Greek coast, highlighting the importance of these guiding beacons for seafarers throughout history.

Outdoor Exhibits: The Aegean Maritime Museum also features several outdoor exhibits, including:

1. Evangelistria: Explore the fully-restored Evangelistria, a traditional wooden sailing ship from the early 20th century, which provides a tangible glimpse into the past and the challenges faced by Aegean sailors.

2. Armenistis Lighthouse: Marvel at the striking, original mechanism of the Armenistis Lighthouse, built in 1890 and once a guiding light for ships passing through the treacherous waters near Mykonos.

Practical Information: The Aegean Maritime Museum is located in the enchanting area of Mykonos Town, within easy walking distance of many popular attractions, shops, and restaurants. The museum is typically open from April to October, with daily operating hours from 10:00 am to 8:00 pm. Admission fees are modest, and group rates are available upon request.

Visit the **website**

Mykonos Map with All Interesting Spots

The map below includes every point of interest mentioned in this guide. Furthermore, includes some museums and other extra sights which you may want to visit if you have some more time or in case you want to alter our recommended itinerary.

Click here to view it on Google Maps or visit bit.ly/mykonosallspots

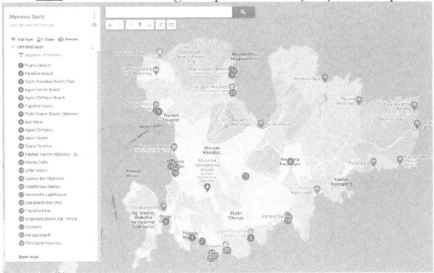

You can also scan the QR code below, if you are an offline reader:

3-Day Itinerary: Mykonos Essentials

Day 1: Arrival and Mykonos Town Exploration

Morning: Arrival and hotel check-in
- Arrive at Mykonos International Airport or Mykonos New Port, depending on your mode of transportation.
- Transfer to your accommodation and check-in. Take some time to freshen up and relax after your journey.

Late morning to afternoon: Explore Mykonos Town (Chora)
- Begin your exploration of Mykonos Town, the island's charming capital, with its narrow streets, white-washed houses, and vibrant bougainvillea.
- Visit the famous Windmills of Mykonos, known as the Kato Mili, which offer a stunning view of the town and the sea.
- Discover the quaint neighborhood of Little Venice, with its colorful houses built right on the water's edge. This is a perfect spot for taking pictures and enjoying the seaside atmosphere.
- Wander through the labyrinthine streets of Chora, stopping at boutiques, art galleries, and local shops to pick up souvenirs or sample local delicacies.

Lunch: Traditional Greek cuisine
- Enjoy lunch at a local taverna, where you can try classic Greek dishes such as moussaka, souvlaki, and fresh seafood.

Afternoon: Explore more of Mykonos Town
- Visit the Church of Panagia Paraportiani, one of the most famous and photographed churches in Mykonos, known for its unique architecture and whitewashed exterior.
- Stroll around the Old Port area and admire the traditional fishing boats and yachts docked in the harbor.

Evening: Sunset and dinner in Mykonos Town
- Head back to Little Venice or the Windmills to watch the spectacular sunset over the Aegean Sea.

- For dinner, choose from a variety of restaurants serving local and international cuisine. Enjoy a leisurely meal while people-watching and soaking in the island atmosphere.

Night: Mykonos nightlife (optional)
- If you're up for it, experience the vibrant nightlife of Mykonos, which is renowned for its lively bars and clubs. Dance the night away, or simply enjoy a cocktail at a trendy bar in the town center.

Day 2: Beach Hopping and Little Venice

Morning: **Beach hopping**
- Start your day with a visit to some of Mykonos' famous beaches. Rent a car, scooter, or take advantage of the local public transportation to explore the island's coastline.
- Begin with a trip to **Platis Gialos**, a popular beach with golden sand and crystal-clear waters. Enjoy a swim, relax on a sunbed, or partake in some water sports activities.
- Next, head to **Psarou Beach**, an upscale spot known for its luxury beach clubs and excellent facilities. Here, you can indulge in a little pampering or simply sunbathe and take in the beautiful surroundings.

Lunch: Beachside dining
- Choose from one of the many beachfront restaurants or cafes in the area for a delicious lunch with a view of the sea. Sample more Greek cuisine, fresh seafood, or international dishes.

Afternoon: More beach hopping
- Continue your beach exploration by visiting **Paraga Beach**, a lively destination with a mix of relaxation and beach parties. Enjoy a refreshing drink at one of the beach bars or take a dip in the turquoise waters.
- End your beach hopping at **Paradise Beach**, known for its stunning beauty and vibrant atmosphere. Relax on the sandy

shores, swim, or participate in water sports like jet-skiing or snorkeling.

Evening: Return to **Little Venice** and dinner
- Head back to Mykonos Town and spend some more time exploring **Little Venice**. Enjoy a drink at one of the waterfront bars, with the colorful buildings and sparkling sea as your backdrop.
- Choose a charming restaurant in the area for dinner, savoring more local flavors and taking in the unique ambiance of Mykonos Town.

Night: Optional nightlife or leisurely evening
- Depending on your preferences, either continue exploring Mykonos' famous nightlife or opt for a more laid-back evening. Stroll through the town's streets, relax at your hotel, or take a moonlit walk along the waterfront.

Day 3: Delos and Rhenia Island Excursion

Morning: Depart for Delos Island
- Start your day early by heading to the Old Port of Mykonos Town to catch a boat to the sacred island of Delos, a UNESCO World Heritage Site.
- Delos is renowned for its archaeological treasures and rich history. As the mythical birthplace of the twin gods Apollo and Artemis, Delos was once a thriving religious and commercial center.

Morning to early afternoon: Explore Delos
- Upon arrival, join a guided tour or explore the island at your own pace. Visit the ancient ruins, including the Terrace of the Lions, the House of Dionysus, and the Delos Archaeological Museum.
- Wander through the well-preserved archaeological site, marveling at the ancient temples, mosaic floors, and the remains of the ancient market.

Lunch: Picnic or onboard dining

- Enjoy a packed picnic lunch on Delos or return to your boat for an onboard meal, depending on your tour package and preferences.

Afternoon: Rhenia Island visit
- After exploring Delos, set sail for the nearby island of Rhenia. Known for its pristine beaches and crystal-clear waters, Rhenia is the perfect place for relaxation and swimming.
- Spend the afternoon lounging on the beach, swimming in the inviting waters, or snorkeling to discover the underwater beauty of the island.

Late afternoon: Return to Mykonos
- As the day comes to an end, board your boat and head back to Mykonos Town. Enjoy the stunning views of the Aegean Sea and the surrounding islands as you make your way back to the island.

Evening: Farewell dinner in Mykonos Town
- For your final night in Mykonos, choose a special restaurant in Mykonos Town to enjoy a farewell dinner. Savor the local flavors one last time, and toast to the memories made during your trip.

Night: Relax or enjoy nightlife (optional)
- Depending on your preferences and energy level, either spend a quiet evening at your hotel or explore more of Mykonos' vibrant nightlife.

A 5-Day Itinerary: Highlights and Hidden Gems

Add to the previous 3-day travel itinerary the following two days' plan:

Day 4: Ano Mera Village and Panormos Beach
Morning: Visit Ano Mera Village

- Begin your day with a visit to the picturesque village of Ano Mera, located in the center of the island. This traditional village offers a glimpse into the authentic life of Mykonos, away from the tourist crowds.
- Explore the village square, lined with quaint cafes and shops, where you can enjoy a morning coffee and sample some local pastries.
- Visit the historic Monastery of Panagia Tourliani, which dates back to the 16th century. Admire its intricate architecture, beautiful bell tower, and the peaceful courtyard.

Lunch: Local cuisine in Ano Mera

- Enjoy lunch at a traditional taverna in Ano Mera, sampling more Greek dishes and experiencing the warm hospitality of the locals.

Afternoon: Relax at Panormos Beach

- After lunch, head to the beautiful Panormos Beach, located on the northern side of the island. This less crowded beach offers a serene atmosphere, with its golden sand and crystal-clear waters.
- Spend the afternoon swimming, sunbathing, or relaxing under the shade of a beach umbrella. If you're up for some adventure, you can also try paddleboarding or snorkeling in the calm waters.
- For those seeking a more exclusive experience, visit the nearby Principote Beach Club, where you can enjoy luxury amenities, comfortable sunbeds, and refreshing cocktails.

Evening: Dinner with a view

- As the sun begins to set, choose a beachside restaurant or return to Mykonos Town for a memorable dinner. Enjoy the delicious local cuisine while taking in the stunning views of the island and the sea.

Night: Stargazing or leisurely evening
- End your day with a leisurely stroll along the beach, watching the stars come out over the Aegean Sea. Alternatively, relax at your hotel, or explore more of Mykonos Town's charming streets and vibrant nightlife, depending on your preferences.

Day 5: Hidden Beaches and Sunset at Armenistis Lighthouse
Morning: Discover hidden beaches
- Start your day by exploring some of Mykonos' lesser-known beaches, away from the bustling tourist spots. Rent a car or scooter to reach these secluded locations, or join a guided tour to uncover these hidden gems.
- Visit **Agios Sostis**, a beautiful, unspoiled beach with golden sand and turquoise waters. This tranquil spot is perfect for swimming, sunbathing, or simply relaxing in a peaceful setting.
- Next, head to **Fokos Beach**, another secluded paradise with crystal-clear waters and a more remote atmosphere. Enjoy the natural beauty and serenity of this beach, away from the crowds.

Lunch: Beachside picnic or taverna
- Pack a picnic lunch to enjoy on the beach, or visit a nearby local taverna to indulge in more traditional Greek cuisine.

Afternoon: More hidden beaches
- Continue your beach exploration by visiting **Kapari Beach**, a small, idyllic cove with soft sand and clear waters, perfect for swimming and snorkeling.
- End your beach tour at **Merchia Beach**, a remote, untouched location accessible only by a dirt road or boat. Immerse yourself in the natural beauty and peaceful ambiance of this pristine beach.

Evening: Sunset at Armenistis Lighthouse
- As the day comes to an end, make your way to the historic **Armenistis Lighthouse**, located on the northwestern tip of

141

Mykonos. This 19th-century lighthouse offers a panoramic view of the surrounding islands and the Aegean Sea.

- Find a comfortable spot to sit and watch the sunset, as the sky turns brilliant shades of orange, pink, and purple. Capture the breathtaking views and create lasting memories of your time in Mykonos.

Night: Dinner and relaxation

- For your final night, choose a cozy restaurant in Mykonos Town or near your accommodation to enjoy a leisurely dinner. Savor the local flavors and reminisce about the highlights of your trip.
- Spend the rest of the evening relaxing at your hotel, strolling through the town, or experiencing Mykonos' vibrant nightlife, depending on your preferences and energy level.

Customizing Your Mykonos Itinerary

10.1 Family-Friendly Options

- Choose accommodations with family-friendly amenities, such as kids' clubs, swimming pools, or playgrounds.
- Visit beaches with calm waters and facilities like sunbeds, umbrellas, and beachside cafes, such as Ornos or Kalafatis Beach.
- Enjoy a day of fun at Mykonos Watermania, a water park with slides, pools, and activities for all ages.
- Take a family-friendly guided tour of Delos Island, where children can learn about Greek mythology and history in an engaging way.

10.2 Romantic Getaways

- Opt for a luxurious boutique hotel or a private villa to enjoy a secluded and romantic stay.
- Arrange a private sailing tour or yacht charter for a day of exploring the coast and nearby islands.
- Experience a romantic dinner at a fine dining restaurant overlooking the sea, such as Bill & Coo, or Scorpios.
- Take a leisurely sunset walk along the waterfront in Little Venice, followed by a cocktail at a cozy bar.

10.3 Adventure Seekers

- Participate in water sports activities, such as windsurfing, kiteboarding, jet-skiing, or scuba diving at beaches like Kalafatis or Ftelia.
- Go off-roading on an ATV or 4x4 vehicle tour to explore the rugged coastline and hidden beaches.
- Try a hiking or biking tour to discover the island's natural beauty and stunning landscapes.

- Experience the thrill of Mykonos' nightlife at popular clubs like Cavo Paradiso, Tropicana, or Super Paradise Beach Club.

10.4 Cultural Enthusiasts

- Dive into the island's history with a guided tour of Delos Island and its archaeological treasures.
- Visit the Aegean Maritime Museum and the Folklore Museum to learn about Mykonos' maritime history and traditional culture.
- Explore the picturesque village of Ano Mera and the Monastery of Panagia Tourliani, where you can get a glimpse into authentic Mykonian life.
- Attend a traditional Greek cooking class or wine tasting experience to immerse yourself in the local flavors and culinary heritage.

How to Get to Mykonos from Santorini

Embarking on a journey to explore the enchanting beauty of the Greek islands, visitors to Mykonos often find themselves eager to discover the equally captivating island of Santorini. In this section, we provide a comprehensive guide for Mykonos visitors on how to seamlessly travel to Santorini, delving into various transportation options, schedules, and insider tips to ensure a smooth and enjoyable journey between these two iconic island destinations. Unravel the mysteries of the Aegean Sea as you venture from the vibrant shores of Mykonos to the mesmerizing caldera views of Santorini, creating unforgettable memories along the way.

Here is all the information on how to get to Mykonos from Santorini, with a ferry (fast ferry or standard ferry), a direct flight or a daily tour.

Santorini to Mykonos with a Ferry

The codename of the port in Santorini is [JTR]. Bear in mind that Santorini is also called "Thira", so when you are searching for the departure port of Santorini on the web you can search for either "Santorini" or "Thira".

This is the port of Santorini [JTR].

The port in Santorini [JTR is the code name]

The codename of the port in Mykonos is [JMK]. Actually Mykonos has two ports. The old port and the new one. But just input "Mykonos" in the port destination on the web and you will find all available ferry routes.

Below you can see the new port of Mykonos. You can see a cruise ship and a fast ferry leaving the port. The new port of Mykonos is around 7 minutes drive time from Mykonos town. You are not advised to walk from Mykonos town to it, as you would need to walk more than 25 minutes under the hot sun.

The new port of Mykonos.

The best site to book your ferry ticket is http://www.viva.gr. It has an english version too. Make sure that you book your travel at least a couple of months before going to Mykonos, if you plan to travel during July or August.

Standard vs Fast Ferries traveling from Santorini to Mykonos: There are two types of ferries traveling from Santorini to Mykonos. The standard ferries (lower price, bigger boats, more time to reach Mykonos, travelling with strong winds) and the fast ferries (higher price, smaller boats, less time to reach Mykonos, note travelling with strong winds). Also, some ferries accept vehicles (cars and motorbikes), while others don't.

How long is the ferry ride from Santorini to Mykonos? The fastest ferry will take you from Santorini to Mykonos in 1hour and 55 minutes. The slowest ferry will take the trip in 4 hours.

The first ferry of the day during the peak season, leaves Santorini at 10:25 in the morning. The last ferry of the day leaves Santorini for Mykonos at 14:30 in the noon.

If you want to go from Santorini to Mykonos during the shoulder season or the low season, there are far less choices. For example, if you want to travel from Santorini to Mykonos in May, there are only four ferries per day, instead of the eight ferries per day that you will find during August. In April, there are only two ferries per day. In October there are six ferries per day.

If there are strong winds (above 6 Bf), some fast ferries don't travel and you will need to change to a standard ferry, which is usually a much bigger ferry which can travel with stronger winds.

Prices and Travel Duration of Ferries From Santorini to Mykonos during the Peak Season of July, August, September

Here are the ferry companies that travel from Santorini to Mykonos during the peak season of July, August and September, with the respective times and costs:

Company	Ferry Name	Duration	Price
Sea Jets	Caldera Vista	3h 5m	54 Euros
Sea Jets	Power Jet	2h 10m	67 Euros
Golden Star Ferries	Superferry II	4h	35 Euros
Minoan Lines	Santorini Palace	2h 35m	N/A
Sea Jets	Champion Jet I	1h 55m	43 Euros
Golden Star Ferries	Supercat	2h 40m	42 Euros

| Golden Star Ferries | SuperRunner | 4h | 52 Euros |

As you can see at the above table, your best option is to get the Champion Jet I from Sea Jets which costs 43 euros and takes 1h and 55 minutes to get you from Santorini to Mykonos.

Prices and Travel Time of Santorini to Mykonos Ferries in May

During May, there are four ferries that travel from Santorini to Mykonos. The all leave from 10:00 to 12:00 in the morning. Here is the information:

Company	Ferry	Duration	Price
Sea Jets	Caldera Vista	3h 5min	55 euros
Sea Jets	PowerJet	1h 55min	67 euros
Golden Star Ferries	Superferry II	3h 15min	35 euros
Sea JEts	Champion Jet I	1h 55 min	67 euros

Photos of Ferries Traveling from Santorini to Mykonos

Champion Jet 1 accepts a maximum of 1000 passengers and 200 vehicles. It is 87 meters long and 26 meters wide and it was constructed in 1997. Champion Jet 1 is a Catamaran, with a maximum speed of 40 knots. Here is a photo.

Champion Jet I will get you from Santorini to Mykonos in 2 hours

Caldera Vista ferry is another popular choice on how to get from Santorini to Mykonos with a fast ferry. Caldera Vista will get you from Santorini to Mykonos in 3 hours

This is the Golden Star Ferries, Super Cat ferry:

And this is the SuperRunner from the Goldenstar Ferries:

Santorini to Mykonos: Ferry or Flight?

There is no direct flight connecting Santorini's airport with Mykonos airport. Olympic Airways has a flight with one stop in Athens, which flies from Santorini to Athens and then from Athens to Mykonos, in 2 hours and 20 minutes and a cost of 102 euros per person.

Obviously, this doesn't make any sense, compared to getting a fast ferry from Santorini to Mykonos, paying 66 euros per person and reaching Mykonos in 2 hours.

So, if you wonder whether you should travel from Santorini to Mykonos with a Ferry or a flight, the answer is clear. Get a standard or fast ferry.

Santorini to Mykonos with a Helicopter

The Helicopter launch pad in Santorini. It takes 40 minutes to get you to Mykonos.

Yes, it is possible to get a helicopter and travel from Mykonos to Santorini. The duration of the flight is 40 minutes, the helicopter can transfer a group of 4 persons and the price is 2.000 euros. So, this is around 500 euros per person. You can book your helicopter ride from Mykonos to Santorini, here.

Santorini to Mykonos with a Private Plane

The private plane from Santorini to Mykonos, will get you in 40 minutes.

Getting a private plane from Santorini to Mykonos, has the same cost with the helicopter ride. The private plane will get you from Santorini to Mykonos in 40 minutes with a cost of 2.000 euros for 4 persons.
Apart from the obvious fact that you will travel in the most luxurious (and expensive) way, getting a private plane or a helicopter from Santorini to Mykonos, gives you the benefit of enjoying the Cyclades islands from the sky.

You can book it your private plane from Santorini to Mykonos, here.

Photography Tips and Iconic Photo Spots

Photography is an essential part of any memorable trip, and Mykonos offers countless stunning photo opportunities. In this section, we provide tips on the best times for photography and some iconic photo spots on the island.

11.1. Best Times for Photography

Golden Hour:
The golden hour is the period shortly after sunrise or just before sunset when the sun casts a warm, soft light on the landscape. This is the ideal time for capturing the beautiful colors and contrasts of Mykonos. The golden hour typically lasts for about an hour, so plan your photography sessions accordingly.

Sunrise:
Sunrise is an excellent time for photography in Mykonos, as it offers both beautiful lighting and fewer tourists. During the early morning hours, you can capture the serene beauty of Mykonos Town or the beaches without the usual daytime crowds. Wake up early and head to your desired photography location to make the most of this peaceful time.

Sunset:
Sunset is another fantastic time for photography, as the sun casts a warm, orange glow over the island. This is the perfect time to capture the classic Mykonos windmills or the iconic Little Venice with its colorful waterfront buildings. Arrive at your chosen location a bit early to ensure you have a good spot to set up your camera.

Blue Hour:
The blue hour occurs just before sunrise and shortly after sunset when the sky takes on a deep blue hue. This is a great time to photograph the island's landmarks, as they are often illuminated against the dramatic

backdrop. The contrast between the warm artificial lights and the cool blue sky can create striking images.

Off-Peak Hours:
Visiting popular sites during off-peak hours can help you avoid the crowds and capture better photos. This may mean heading to the beach early in the morning or visiting Mykonos Town in the late afternoon when the crowds have thinned out. By avoiding peak times, you'll have more space to work with and can focus on capturing the perfect shot.

11.2. Iconic Photo Locations

Mykonos is filled with picturesque locations, and some spots are particularly iconic for capturing the essence of the island. Here are some of the top photo locations you won't want to miss:

1. Windmills of Kato Mili: The famous windmills in Mykonos Town are a must-visit photo location. These historic structures offer a stunning backdrop, especially during sunrise or sunset. From this elevated spot, you can also capture panoramic views of the town and harbor.
2. Little Venice: This colorful, waterfront neighborhood in Mykonos Town is perfect for photography. The vibrant buildings and the sea crashing against the shore create a beautiful, romantic atmosphere. Capture the charm of Little Venice during sunset, when the sun casts a warm glow on the buildings.
3. Panagia Paraportiani Church: This iconic church complex is a fascinating subject for photography. The unique architecture and whitewashed walls contrast beautifully against the bright blue sky. Visit during the golden hour or blue hour to create visually striking images.
4. Mykonos Town (Chora): The narrow, winding streets of Mykonos Town are filled with white-washed buildings, colorful doors, and vibrant bougainvillea. Wander through the alleys to discover

countless photo opportunities, capturing the charm and character of this picturesque town.

5. Super Paradise Beach: This popular beach boasts crystal-clear waters and golden sands, making it an ideal location for beach photography. Arrive early in the morning to avoid the crowds and capture the serene beauty of the shoreline.

6. Armenistis Lighthouse: Located at the northern tip of the island, this historic lighthouse offers breathtaking views of the surrounding seascape. It's an ideal spot for landscape photography and capturing stunning sunsets.

7. Agios Sostis Beach: This secluded beach provides a beautiful, natural setting for photography. With its unspoiled landscape and calm waters, Agios Sostis is perfect for capturing the untouched beauty of Mykonos.

8. Ano Mera Village: Venture out to this traditional village to photograph a more authentic side of Mykonos. Capture images of the historic Panagia Tourliani Monastery, quaint village streets, and friendly locals going about their daily lives.

9. Delos Island: As a UNESCO World Heritage site, Delos Island is an important archaeological location filled with ancient ruins. Take a day trip from Mykonos to photograph the impressive ruins, such as the Terrace of the Lions and the House of Dionysus.

10. Viewpoints: Mykonos has several elevated spots that offer panoramic views of the island and its surroundings. For example, the hill near the windmills is an excellent spot for capturing wide-angle shots of Mykonos Town and the sparkling Aegean Sea.

By visiting these iconic photo locations, you'll be able to capture the stunning beauty and unique character of Mykonos, preserving your memories of this enchanting island.

Thank You!

As you conclude your Mykonos travel guide, we hope that the suggested itineraries and customized options have provided you with inspiration for an unforgettable trip to this enchanting Greek island. Mykonos truly has something for everyone, whether you are seeking relaxation, romance, adventure, or cultural experiences. With its beautiful beaches, charming towns, rich history, and vibrant nightlife, Mykonos is an ideal destination for travelers of all tastes and preferences.

As you plan your trip, remember to consider your personal interests and priorities, as well as the time of year and local events. No matter which itinerary you choose or how you customize your journey, Mykonos is sure to leave you with lasting memories and a desire to return to explore even more of its hidden gems and captivating allure.

Safe travels, and enjoy your Mykonos adventure!

Your friends at Guidora.

Guidora Mykonos in 3 Days Travel Guide ©

Disclaimer

The publishers have checked the information in this travel guide, but its accuracy is not warranted or guaranteed. Mykonos visitors are advised that opening times should always be checked before making a journey.

Tracing Copyright Owners

Every effort has been done to trace the copyright holders of referred material. Where these efforts have not been successful, copyright owners are invited to contact the Editor (Guidora) so that their copyright can be acknowledged and/or the material removed from the publication.

Creative Commons Content

We are most grateful to publishers of Creative Commons material, including images. Our policies concerning this material are (1) to credit the copyright owner, and provide a link where possible (2) to remove Creative Commons material, at once, if the copyright owner so requests - for example, if the owner changes the licensing of an image.

We will also keep our interpretation of the Creative Commons Non-Commercial license under review. Along with, we believe, most web publishers, our current view is that acceptance of the 'Non-Commercial' condition means (1) we must not sell the image or any publication containing the image (2) we may, however, use an image as an illustration for some information which is not being sold or offered for sale.

Note to other copyright owners

We are grateful to those copyright owners who have given permission for their material to be used. Some of the material comes from secondary and tertiary sources. In every case, we have tried to locate the original author or photographer and make the appropriate acknowledgment. In some cases, the sources have proved obscure, and we have been unable to track them down. In these cases, we would like to hear from the copyright owners and will be pleased to acknowledge them in future editions or remove the material.

Printed in Great Britain
by Amazon